buy*in

JOHN P. KOTTER
AND LORNE A. WHITEHEAD

buy * in

*saving your
good idea
from getting
shot down

We've been successful, why
Money (or some other proble
ddress) is the only real iss
failing!! What's the h
d that, and this, and
proposal doesn't g
gg problem. We
You can't have it

It's just too much wo
work here, we're diff
a slippery slope. We c
never convince enough
not equipped to do th
to work. No one else
have it both ways.
didn't work. W

didn't   o
d. Goo   he
n't wor   e
a slippe   We
ou'll never
We're simply not   d   o far. You hav
s too simplistic to   oblem. You'
e else does this.   values. It's
                               o one else does
                               car   on't work.

Harvard Business Review Press
Boston, Massachusetts

Library of Congress Cataloging-in-Publication Data

Kotter, John P., 1947-
    Buy-in : saving your good idea from being shot down / John P.
Kotter and Lorne A. Whitehead.
       p. cm.
    ISBN 978-1-4221-5729-9 (hardcover : alk. paper)   1. Sales
promotion.   2. Creative ability in business.   3. Public relations.
I. Whitehead, Lorne A.   II. Title.
    HF5438.5.K686 2010
    650.1—dc22

                                                    2010016497

The paper used in this publication meets the requirements
of the American National Standard for Permanence of Paper
for Publications and Documents in Libraries and Archives
Z39.48-1992.

contents

preface

We have all experienced the basic problem addressed here, and in a very personal way, because it is an old, common, human, and increasingly important problem.

You believe in a good idea. You're convinced it is needed badly, and needed now. But you can't make it happen on your own. You need sufficient support in order to implement it and make things better. You or your allies present the plan. You present it well. Then, along with thoughtful issues being raised, come the confounding questions, inane comments, and verbal bullets—either directly at you or, even worse, behind your back. It matters not that the idea is needed, insightful, innovative, and logical. It matters not if the issues involved are extremely important to a business, an individual, or even a nation. The proposal is still shot down, or is accepted but without sufficient support to gain all of its true benefits, or slowly dies a sad death.

It can be maddening. You end up flustered, embarrassed, or furious. All those who would benefit from the idea lose. You lose. In an extreme case, a whole company or nation may lose. And, as we shall demonstrate in this book, it doesn't have to be that way.

The competent creation and implementation of good ideas is a basic life skill, relevant to the twenty-one-year-old college graduate, the fifty-five-year-old corporate CEO, and virtually everyone else. This skill, or the lack of it, affects the economy, governments, families, and most certainly our own lives.

The challenge is that the amount of thought and education put into creating good ideas is far higher today than the knowledge and instruction on how to implement those ideas. In the world of business, for example, the field of strategy has made huge advances in the past twenty years. The field of strategy implementation, in contrast, has made much less progress.

It would be wonderful if the good ideas you champion, on or off the job, could simply stand on their own. But far too often, this is not the case. Whether it's a big bill before Congress, an innovative corporate strategy, or tonight's plan for dinner and the movies, sensible ideas can be ignored, shot down, or, more often, wounded so badly that they produce little gain. A wounded idea might still get 51 percent of the relevant heads nodding approval. But when true buy-in is thin, the smallest of obstacles can eventually derail a supposedly agreed-upon proposal.

This is not a book about persuasion and communication in general, or even about all the useful methods people use to create buy-in. Instead, here we offer a single method that can be unusually powerful in building strong support for a good idea, a method that is rarely used or used well and that does not require blinding rhetorical skills or charismatic magic.

The method is counterintuitive in a number of ways. It does not try to keep naysayers out of the room. Just the opposite, it welcomes them into the discussion of a new proposal and virtually encourages them to shoot at you. It doesn't try to build a power base or use a powerful personality to steamroller over the unfair opposition. It actually treats the unfair, illogical, and sneaky with a large degree of respect. It doesn't try to overwhelm attackers, or preempt their advance, with selling-selling-selling, complex manipulations, or long, logical lists of reasons-reasons-reasons. Instead, it responds to attacks in ways that are always simple, clear, crisp, and filled with common sense.

We have seen that this counterintuitive method of walking into the fray, showing respect for all, and using simple, clear, and commonsense responses can not only keep good ideas from getting shot down but can actually turn attacks *to your advantage* in capturing busy peoples' attention, helping them grasp an idea, and ultimately building strong buy-in.

The ideas and advice offered here are not based on a hypothetical theory or just our opinion. They are based in part on extensive observation by Lorne Whitehead in his roles over the years as an entrepreneur, an executive, an administrator, and a professor of physics at the University of British Columbia. They are also grounded in an ongoing flow of research by John Kotter at Harvard Business

School and his work on the topics of leadership and change, published largely in four books: *Leading Change, The Heart of Change, Our Iceberg Is Melting,* and *A Sense of Urgency.* And while preparing this work, the authors also collected and incorporated numerous related observations provided by colleagues.

We present these ideas first with a story of a face-to-face meeting, where a brave few describe and defend an idea in a crowd of seventy-five, in a room, over a few hours. It is one specific setting, but we have found that the attacks shown in the story can be seen anywhere, and the best method for responding works anywhere: with back-and-forth e-mails across continents; ten people at lunch or in a classroom; a paper sent to a thousand employees; a series of two or twenty-two meetings; or dueling memos.

In part 2 of the book, we become analytical, showing explicitly what was happening in the story, discussing four common attack strategies, and explaining our method. We show the twenty-four generic and maddening attacks people often use, along with an effective response to each. We provide a few more examples of how this all plays itself out in real situations. We end with clear, straightforward advice on how to easily use this material, since, though we think our method is intellectually fascinating, our goal here is entirely practical: to help you save your good ideas from being shot down; to help you get the relevant people to strongly buy into an idea (or even a grand vision), no matter how difficult; and to help you make the rapid change in your world not only a hazard, but also an opportunity.

In the appendix, we explain the method within the context of efforts to produce large-scale change—an increasingly important topic Kotter has been studying for two decades. If you are involved in, or particularly interested in, large-scale change, you might be well served to glance at that material after you finish this preface and before starting the book.

For ease of reading, we have made our story, the issues, and the setting as uncomplicated as we can without losing the complexity of our subject. This has led us to a story of a public meeting in a small town library, concerning new computers. You are left to translate this example into contexts specifically relevant to you and to modes of interaction other than from public gatherings of a particular size: perhaps a lunch, an e-mail, a report, a videoconference, a meeting in the hallway. Trust us; you can make that translation.

We will spare you the details from neurology, psychology, and elsewhere that explain why a story can be a powerful learning mechanism, more powerful for most people than any analytical treatment. Let's just say that we hope you will find our story engaging, memorable, whimsical, and fun. But as you read the Centerville Library tale, don't underestimate the deep seriousness of either the subject or our intent. Whimsy is a means, not an end.

—John Kotter
  Lorne Whitehead

the
centerville
story

part one

y change?
em a proposal
sue. You're implying
hidden agenda here?
d that...? Your proposal
go far enough. You
can't afford to do that.
t both ways.

ork to do this. Won't
fferent. It puts us on
can't afford this. You'll
h people. We're sim
his. It's too simp
e does this. You
. Tried that bef
Ve can't afford

1.

the death
of a good plan

Your pulse is racing. Your turn is next, and public speaking isn't your favorite activity. You serve on the Citizens Advisory Committee for Centerville Library. The committee is meeting right now in open forum, which means anyone the library serves can attend the session, and about seventy-five people, in total, fill the room.

The chair is about to ask for your presentation. Earlier this month, you agreed to bring forward a plan for endorsement this evening. It's a proposal devised by you and some supporters of the library, one of whom is the manager of a prominent local company.

The proposal is simple. Centerville Library can't afford the twenty-five to thirty new computers it needs, much less up-to-date printers and networking and other support equipment (like computer-friendly, ergonomic chairs). The total cost, at retail, would eat up a huge chunk of its very tight budget. But the local computer store, Centerville Computers, has agreed to help. It has offered that for the next three months, for every six Centerville families that buy a new computer from it, Centerville Computers will donate one state-of-the-art, big-screen, new computer to the library, along with sufficient printers, networking, chairs—everything you could dream of.

The proposal is a rare opportunity that makes total sense for the library and the town. The facts and logic are compelling. It clearly will help the library take a big step into the twenty-first century, especially since you can't see how you would be able to find funds for this in next year's budget or in the year after next. It will assist librarians. It will benefit the less affluent kids in town who need, but don't have, easy access to good computers. Now the task is just to convince others, get their support, and move forward to execute the plan—and quickly, before Centerville Computers walks away.

Centerville Computers will need to get approval from its head office, and the library board will need to approve the commercial aspect of this donation as well, but the board almost certainly will do so as long as the plan is endorsed at this public meeting of the Citizens Advisory Committee. Unfortunately, the timing is tight—you need this endorsement tonight in order to get the approvals in time for the year-end buying season. Otherwise, the plan won't work.

You feel particularly strongly about the proposal—strongly enough to do the public speaking that you don't much like—because you know these easy-to-access computers would so benefit the less affluent children in town. Most can get to the library easily using public transportation. Many cannot easily reach the schools they are bused to, and the schools have shorter hours and are not open on the weekend. For the more affluent children, this is not a problem. They have computers at home, within a few feet of their rooms, if not in their rooms, and available whenever they want, seven days a week. Anyone in the next generation who is not highly computer literate is going to have a hard time in life. Failing to help everyone with this challenge, or worse yet not even trying to help, doesn't strike you as making any sense for the economy, the town, employers, or the children. For all these reasons, you've developed a deep, personal belief in this project; you really *need* its approval this evening.

When it's your turn to speak, you make a brief presentation and then ask for questions and comments before making a formal motion. There are a few minor, good-natured questions, and then it happens. Pompus Meani raises his hand and begins to speak.

Here's the thing about Pompus Meani: he usually values self-importance above doing good. He has been on the Citizens Advisory Committee for a long time, and at least his behavior is consistent. If something will make him seem wiser and more important,

The characters

Not their real names (obviously).
But given the way they often behave,
they might as well be called

—Pompus Meani   —Heidi Agenda

—Avoidus Riski   —Spaci Cadetus

—Allis Welli   —Lookus Smarti

—Divertus Attenti   —Bendi Windi

Your brother-in-law Hank

and you!

---

he supports it. And if not, he opposes it, sometimes stealthily and sometimes flamboyantly as a show of power. He wants to be elected chair of the committee later this year. Even though you have no interest in that role, Pompus sees you as a threat and wants you to look foolish.

He begins by faintly praising your efforts (you *have* worked really hard on this, by the way), and then he utters the dreaded word, "*but* . . . " In a serious, earnest-sounding voice, he says something worrisome, and a few heads nod. He adds another problematic comment, and others look both surprised and concerned. Finally, he makes a motion to defer this matter until it has been possible to consider his concerns carefully and properly. The motion is seconded.

Your known supporters, at least a dozen people in the room, actually fear Pompus, offer no comment, and just look to you. And you've got . . . nothing! You just don't have a satisfactory response at your fingertips. You mumble that it will be very unfortunate to have such a delay as it may kill the project, which, you say, is a terrible mistake. But with the motion seconded, a vote must be held. The majority, around 55 percent, vote for deferral, and the plan is dead. All your work has gone up in smoke. An important opportunity to help the kids and the library and the town is lost. You feel embarrassed and incredibly frustrated. And you must restrain yourself from a maddening impulse to strangle Pompus Meani.

So what did Pompus say? And what could you have said in response? These are questions related to one of life's more fundamental skills, to crucial capabilities for those trying to transform institutions in an age of rapid change, and to abilities that, when missing, can leave us emotionally distraught, no matter the setting or our role in that setting.

Attacks that derail good ideas can come from all sorts of people, not just Pompus Meanis. For example, Pompus has a cousin, Heidi Agenda, whom you admire, but who has an undisclosed personal reason for opposing the plan—a reason that is more important to her than fairness or your friendship. Furthermore, there is always Bendi Windi, who usually blows with the wind and may, without really trying to be mean, say your plan is bad just so she can fit in. And there are others to take into account, such as Avoidus Riski, Divertus Attenti, and Lookus Smarti, whose most common traits will be left for now to the reader's imagination.

Of course, Avoidus and the lot live not only in Centerville. They are all around us. You have seen them many times before and will surely see them many times in the future. You will encounter them in a meeting, in an attack on your memo, in a telephone call between Houston and Hamburg, in your school, or (perhaps) in your own family. We see this behavior on and off the job. Even *you* (gasp) might behave as they do some of the time. When the issues are small—with minor encounters that happen weekly if not daily—the Pompuses of the world can cause frustration and embarrassment, but such feelings quickly pass. However, when the issues are *not* small, the loss of a good idea can create consequences that can linger for a very long time.

In some ways, it is a shame we even need a book like this. But we do—first, because our requirement to implement good ideas is a central part of what life is all about; second, because in an era of increasing change, the number of new plans or strategies we need is growing; third, because genuinely good ideas are damaged or killed all the time for all sorts of reasons; and fourth, because a most fundamental and powerful solution to this problem is not at all obvious: *that to get people to truly buy into a new idea, you can go into the arena, armed with the knowledge in this book, and encourage them, not stop them, from sending in the lions.*

One important caveat: we are not talking here about the *creation* of good ideas—the gathering of information, brainstorming, or the process of generating new proposals. Much has been written on these issues, and we take that as a given. Here we focus on how you keep those ideas from being shot down and how you build sufficiently strong support around them so that successful action follows.

But enough for now. Let us go back to Centerville and let the meeting begin again. Unlike in the real world, this time you and the others who created the proposal will have a second chance. And this time, you will be hit by confusing, sneaky, and illogical commentary that can undermine essential support for any smart idea. These generic behaviors, seen so often in real life, will be devilishly hard to deal with, partly because they can sound so sincere, or reasonable, or logical. So get ready, because it will be brutal, indeed much tougher than we normally see in reality. And this time . . . well, you'll see.

2.

saving the day in centerville, part one

This time, we begin our story the evening before the town meeting. The proposal is so sensible that it should sell itself. But you find yourself writing notes and more notes, which should make you feel more prepared and thus confident. But they don't. Then a little light bulb goes off in your head, and you think of Hank.

Hank is your brother-in-law. Unlike some of the people you know who aren't particularly enthusiastic about their brothers-in-law, you have always liked Hank. He is both intelligent and a genuinely good person. He also has had considerable experience in dealing with groups of people, small and large, inside businesses and elsewhere. He is plainspoken but, from what you have seen, very sharp.

You call him. When he suggests that instead of a phone conversation, he would be willing to come over to your house, you accept his offer enthusiastically.

Upon arrival, and after a few pleasantries, Hank asks you to brief him. You do. Computers and support equipment are really needed, yet that would require a large expenditure for the library, which has a limited budget this year, the next one, or for who knows how long. Centerville Computers has offered to help in the following way, and so on.

He is impressed with the proposal. He hadn't even heard of it, making you wonder how many other people in town haven't, either. Hank asks what you have already done to explain it and get support from others. You tell him. The group behind the proposal has sent a brief description of the idea along with the invitation to the meeting tomorrow night to the many hundreds of people who use the library. The group members have given some thought to who might object and why. Two of the proposal's supporters are prepared to make carefully planned comments from the audience when you go into a question-and-answer period.

Hank nods as you talk. When you stop, he explains that he has actually thought much, over his long career, about why his best ideas either soared or were shot down. He says he has often wondered why his bosses', neighbors', and friends' good ideas have been supported and implemented in some cases, but in others were ignored, or left crushed on the pavement.

Hank points out that there are many ways to poke holes in any simple plan or complex change, but—don't panic—most are very easy to deal with because people have their facts wrong. For example: "The computer store will raise its prices as soon as we okay this proposal!" Response: "A part of the deal we made is that last week's prices are set in cement for the duration of this program." Such objections can be a little more difficult to diplomatically overcome if the objector has thought carefully about your idea, yet misunderstood a subtle point. But if you have clarity of the facts and the logic, you just explain, and do so as clearly and simply as possible. For a reasonable person, the response will work. Actually, having to think through the facts and logic before presenting an idea is always useful since you may find it's not such a good idea!

But—Hank says—there are a handful of distinct and familiar types of questions, concerns, and outright attacks that are used against new ideas everywhere and are surprisingly tricky to deal with in "real time," no matter how sound the idea. These are little bombs that cannot be defused with a few facts, or bullets that can so fluster you that your response creates problems instead of solving them.

He reminds you of an old and politically incorrect joke, where a cunning reporter asks a young nominee for an important judicial position, "Sir, have you stopped beating your wife?" The poor soul stammers, "No, yes, I mean . . . " and the evening news clip is complete, whereas an experienced person might smile and calmly respond, "It's well known that I've always been kind and respectful to everyone, most certainly including my rather formidable spouse."

Hank says that a "beating your wife" question, thrown at a fine young candidate for public office, may seem so ridiculous as to be unworthy of serious discussion. But there are very real assaults—made verbally or in written statements—that can be equally bizarre or stupid, yet have the capacity to seriously trip you up if you are not well prepared. Because these "attacks" are used often and widely, anyone wishing to impede a proposal probably has seen them and their potential power. Fortunately, Hank says, they can all be dealt with if you are prepared and the audience isn't too nasty.

Hank patiently goes through a typical scenario. You listen, literally leaning forward on the edge of your seat. Then he continues with scenario after scenario. "Someone says the proposal does not go far enough," he tells you. "A good response is . . . Someone asks why he or she should risk a change since the person has been so successful in the past. A good response is . . ." When he runs out of thoughts, he takes a break to find something to drink. Then after a few minutes, he starts again with a few more attacks and effective responses. You anxiously take notes. When he runs out of observations, you look at your notes and find *about two dozen ways* in which others might crush your computer proposal and two dozen responses that can save the day. Twenty-four sounds like a *very long* list.

The two of you talk about the opposition you might encounter at your meeting and who might be the opposers. He takes his list of twenty-four attacks and asks you which might come out tomorrow night. You consider the question and offer ideas. He takes the generic responses to these likely attacks and helps you think about more specific responses.

The time flies by—7:00 p.m. becomes 10:00 p.m. before you know it. The discussion is enormously educational. It also produces an *unusual mixture of strong feelings*.

On the one hand, it's disturbing. Of his two dozen questions and statements that can undermine support for any good idea, without his help you were able to think of effective responses to *six*. As you begin to panic, Hank says that he'd be surprised if many people can even think of six.

That didn't help.

However, Hank tells you that the confounding, unfair, sneaky, and illogical attacks he has seen over the years are based on only a few strategies. He takes your pad of paper and writes a word, pauses to think, writes a few more words, then stops. You look at the pad and see these items:

—Confusion

—Death by delay

—Fear mongering

—Ridicule and character assassination

15

Attacks that *confuse*, he tells you, sink a good idea by so muddling a conversation in peoples' minds, they begin to wonder if your proposal really makes sense. *Death by delay*, as the name suggests, means raising what seem like logical concerns that will require so much time to sort out that a proposal is no longer relevant or feasible. *Fear-mongering* attacks push emotional hot buttons that raise anxieties. *Ridicule* and *character assassination* go after the person defending the idea, not the idea itself. Hank says that people who use these strategies range from individuals who are honestly trying to make sure a good decision is made, to people who are anxious, self-centered, very manipulative, or angry. Often it's hard to even guess what others' motives are.

Hank then writes a few more words on your pad—again starting, pausing to think, then writing more—and hands you back his pen. You look and see:

- Don't be afraid of distracters. Handled correctly, they can actually help you!

- Always respond in ways that are simple, straightforward, and honest.

- Show respect for everyone.

- Watch the audience (not just the people shooting at you).

- Anticipate and prepare for attacks in advance.

In his experience, Hank tells you, that's all that people basically do to communicate and defend proposals in order to win sufficient buy-in.

A simple response can fight confusion and delays. Straightforwardness undermines character assassination. Respect prompts, in return, respect for you and your idea. A constant eye on the audience whose support you need keeps you from making the dangerous mistake of focusing only on the aggravating disruptors. Preparation helps you anticipate how people might totally confuse the conversation, kill your idea through delay, raise too many anxieties, or effectively ridicule you and other supporters so that your credibility, and message, die. And, he says, the act of jumping into the fray, walking up to the lions instead of running away, can actually turn attacks to your advantage, as long as you are respectful, crisp, sensitive to the entire audience, and so on.

You ask many questions. Hank answers them, sometimes very clearly and sometimes (or at least it seems to you) not so clearly. His final point about letting the "lions" come after you is unclear and unnerving. So you become somewhat anxious once again.

It all seems a bit much. You tell Hank that you wish you could have seen him dealing with this sort of situation at least *once*. And then it hits you.

Why not ask the chair of the Citizens Advisory Committee to let Hank make the presentation and answer the questions? It only takes you a few moments to decide that this is a *very good idea*.

You ask Hank. He shakes his head. Some of the people in the room will know he has not worked to develop the proposal, and they will, quite naturally, wonder why he is explaining it. Someone opposing the plan could use this fact to his or her advantage, and the meeting could quickly go off track. He doesn't say so, but it does occur to you that he may also be reluctant because public speaking is not his favorite activity, either.

Nevertheless, you don't retreat. After some back-and-forth, Hank reluctantly agrees to a four-part deal: (1) you make the presentation, (2) you start the Q&A by asking a few of your supporters to speak, (3) then you turn it over to Hank with (4) the provision that if he needs you to supply the relevant facts, you will be sitting at the head table with him.

You immediately call the chair of the Citizens Advisory Committee. Understandably, he is not thrilled with the idea of inserting Hank at this late stage. But with some effort, you win the argument (probably because the committee head picks up the near panic in your voice).

You wish you could have another week. Hank had stressed the virtue of preparation, and you think of all the ways you could lay the groundwork for a smooth performance at the meeting.

You tell all this to Hank and he shrugs. "You play the hand you're dealt." And you need to be careful about orchestrating events behind the scenes, he warns. If seen, it might feel to others like manipulation. It's hard to find folks who like being manipulated.

As he leaves, you thank him profusely for helping out with your problem. He smiles and says, "Actually, it may be a good problem." Before you can ask him what that means, he is gone.

* * *

All day today, you can't stop thinking about the meeting. You leave work at 5:15 and have a sandwich for dinner. Most people arrive at the town hall around 7:00 p.m. You are there at 6:40. Hank is not there yet (mild panic). But at 6:45, he is in the hall, too. Richard, the chair of the Citizens Advisory Committee, calls the session to order at 7:15.

There are about seventy-five people in the audience. To you, it seems like four hundred. A head table faces the crowd with seats for Hank, you, Richard (a long-time library supporter), Jane (who probably did more of the work than anyone else to put the proposal together), and Melinda (a high school student who may have inspired the computer store to come up with this proposal).

After a few general comments, Richard turns the meeting over to you.

You know the problem, the opportunity, and the specific proposal very well. A change is clearly needed at the library. To help the people of Centerville, the library needs many new computers and printers. There is not enough money in the library's budget—not even close—for the needed new technology. But there is a solution to the problem. The local computer store will provide one free workstation, with supporting printers, and even state-of-the-art tables and chairs, for every six comparable computers people purchase at regular prices over the next three months. This can help the librarians, the people who use the library, and those less-than-affluent kids, one of whom is the junior member of the group, Melinda. She sits two chairs to your left.

Your presentation is short. Hank said the basic idea needs to be presented clearly in just a few minutes. He said to start with the problem or opportunity. Explain why your idea best deals with the problem, emphasizing, in this case, that no one has found another way to fund the purchase of all those new computers. He said to think of the issues that people commonly have raised when you have described the proposal to them. Give the audience your best response to each issue. You follow his plan with the aid of hand-scribbled notes made over a long lunch break.

You finish and look up. A number of people are nodding. Two friends, very visible in the second row, are smiling. No one seems to have a rock in hand ready to throw at you.

You ask George, then Jessica, both of whom worked on creating the proposal, to stand up from their seats in the audience and say a few words. They do so, each stressing the logic of some aspect of the plan. When Jessica finishes her short speech, you think the case has been made clearly and solidly. It certainly feels good to have three of you talking about the obvious merits of the plan, not just you alone.

You turn and nod to the chair of the Citizens Advisory Committee. He commends your group for having several members speak and notes that the newest member, Hank, has been given the last job of facilitating the question period—perhaps he drew the short straw, or is this an initiation rite? There are a few awkward chuckles as Hank stands up in front of about seventy-five residents of Centerville. You sit down beside him to his left.

Hank has what appears to be a few pages of notes on the table in front of him. He looks up.

You search for another known supporter of the proposal. After a moment or two, Allis Welli raises her hand. You look for other hands in the air. There are none.

ALLIS HAS LIVED IN THE TOWN for many years and has been involved in civic affairs, on and off, for decades. She is quite sharp and clearly affluent (on her left hand this evening is a diamond ring slightly smaller than a soccer ball) and she has a reputation among many of those who know her well as having never seen a new idea she particularly liked.

You rub your forehead. She speaks: "I see the merits of this proposal. They have been well explained. But a fundamental problem has not been addressed. And I am concerned that it is a very large problem."

She looks from left to right at the people around her. Your neck tenses.

"First of all, though no one has said so, this is an advertising stunt. I suppose there is nothing wrong with that per se, but the library has never been involved in this sort of . . . "—she looks to you as if she is sucking on a lemon—"arrangement before."

You see at least two people nod. Your heart sinks a few inches.

"Second, I can't imagine that we have ever allowed a supplier of any sort to *dictate* what we should buy—which, as I understand it, is what the computer store is doing here. Can you imagine publishers telling us which books we must purchase?"

She looks at you. You consider explaining why the equipment, although indeed specified by Centerville Computers, is appropriate for the library. You open your mouth, and while you search for words and have trouble finding them, Hank gives you a look that you think means no.

Good. You close your mouth.

Allis continues. "Now, these may sound like two issues of less-than-profound consequence, but they need to be looked at in light of the history of the library and how it has successfully operated." She takes a deep breath. "For those of you who have not lived here for long, I suspect you may not know much about the library. It is a rather amazing history. Fifteen years ago, it won an award from the state's ALA chapter. A few years before that, Richard Coles donated a collection of original-edition Dickens books. How often does that happen?"

A few more nods from people in the audience.

"When the library building was first constructed, it won a major architectural award."

That would have been before you, and everyone else in the room, had been born.

"Here is my point. We have a *process* for how we operate, how we use our resources, who we deal with and how, and this has worked exceptionally well for decades. And I see no evidence that there is anything fundamentally wrong with it today. But with this proposal, we sweep it away."

She sits.

Someone else speaks up: "She has a point there. Should we really try a public-private partnership if we have never done that before?"

Your study group spent hours thinking through the issue of public-private partnerships, and you summarized your conclusions in your opening remarks. Or you meant to. Or you did a crummy job.

Allis stands once again, begins talking, and looks very much in charge. She comes at the proposal from the left, then the right, but her basic theme remains the same: the library has been very successful, thank you, so why risk a change for a few bucks' worth of computers (which she probably will never use)?

Your mind races as you try to think—not the easiest of tasks with dozens of people now looking at Hank, *and you.*

You marvel at how Allis appears to have just said that a process that has led to broken computers is good because the library once won an award! Why would anyone listen to this? ...

But—it requires only a glance at the audience to see that people *are* listening, and no one seems to be ready to throw a tomato at Allis.

You quickly look at Hank and wonder what he is going to do. Clearly, with his philosophy about how to handle situations like this, he won't say, "Oh, Allis, shut up!" And, although the idea has emotional appeal, you do realize it wouldn't be effective or fair. Allis is just being Allis.

You try to clear your head and think. Hank could, you suppose, dig into what Allis's beloved "process" is and try to explain why, at least in this case, it is not appropriate. But the mind boggles thinking of all the possible ways that this discussion could go (the term *death by delay* floats through your head). Allis has been living in the town for decades. She probably knows more about its history, and the library's, than you or Hank or half the room. So Hank could seem uninformed or, even worse, start to look silly (and easily ridiculed). And how should you measure "success" for a library? Talk about a topic that could create arguments and end up totally confusing! So ... maybe ... but ...

Finally, Allis stops her lecture and sits down. You wish that she were in Philadelphia. Or maybe Osaka.

You look at Hank and feel relieved that he—and not you—is fielding questions. "Allis," Hank says, "your point is an interesting one."

She looks at him suspiciously. So do you.

"Yet, we must keep in mind that the world is changing. We see examples of this all the time. In public libraries, I suspect few if any aren't faced with funding problems. I would be surprised if any aren't struggling with the increasing costs of books or new electronic communications."

Jane, who is sitting to your left and who has invested so much time and energy into putting together the proposal, nods vigorously.

"With all the change," asks Hank, "isn't it really more dangerous to automatically hold on to all our historical practices, no matter how fundamental or seemingly successful they have been? Isn't it reasonable to assume that past practices, operating under new circumstances, won't produce the same results? Don't we have to try to adapt? We won't always get it right on the first try. But in a case like this, where things are clearly changing—funding, costs, electronics, and the like—isn't it reasonable to assume that not changing how the library operates can create more problems than taking some actions that are new?"

His questions hang in the air. You wait for more. And wait. But . . . he gives no more.

Allis has her eyes closed, her eyebrows up, and the hand with the soccer-ball ring resting gently on her left cheek. Then her eyes pop open and she starts to race into a monologue on history, process, partnerships, and more. You have trouble following it all, start to make notes, and then find you can't write fast enough.

Hank stands expressionless, mostly looking at Allis, but occasionally panning the room with his eyes. After a minute, certainly no more than two, he says, "Allis." She doesn't stop. He says, "Allis," slightly louder. She slows, then stops, as if to breathe. Hank says, "You raise many points that, I believe, the committee also discussed."

Hank looks at Jane, whose head bobs vigorously up and down. Hank shifts his attention back to Allis.

"I suspect that we could go through those issues, one at a time, for the next hour. But I'm not sure that's practical or necessary. And the fundamental issue wouldn't change, no matter how long we talked. Yes, we have never done anything quite like this in the past, and yes, things have worked out well in the past. But the world of libraries is changing, and we all know that those who fail to adapt eventually become less and less successful."

Allis opens her mouth, but before she can speak, someone to her right says, "No one can argue with that, so let's move on. There are more questions, and we have limited time tonight."

You quickly look left and right, then left and right again. One of Hank's principles was to always watch the crowd, not just a troublesome speaker. The goal, he had said rather firmly, is not to win the hearts and minds of all those who disagree with a proposal, some of whom—for all sorts of reasons—will never be won over, even if they are perfectly good, sensible people. The goal is to win the hearts and minds of the majority, and not just 51 percent. Even the best ideas, he said, can become bogged down, despite "support" from "most" people.

As you quickly pan the audience, you can tell from their expressions that people have not been wowed by Hank's rather simple response. But you see any number of them nodding and only two or three looking particularly grumpy (Allis being the most prominent).

Hank says to Allis, "Since it is a very fundamental issue, it's useful to raise it. Thanks, Allis."

BEFORE YOU CAN BEGIN TO PROCESS what just happened, three hands shoot up. One belongs to Divertus Attenti, who stands without Hank's calling on him.

Divertus says, "Lookus Smarti has told me that there are four good libraries in this state that have no computers at all. *Not one!*"

Divertus stops for a second and nods to Lookus, then continues. "Shouldn't we be examining our *real* problems, especially our lack of money for the basics: books, building maintenance, librarian salaries, and the like? Lookus [another nod to Mr. Smarti] calculates . . . "

Divertus pulls a piece of paper out of his coat jacket.

"We spend about thirty-one point five percent less per citizen than do most towns to our south, and maybe . . . "

He squints while looking at the paper.

" . . . twenty-seven point two percent less than our neighbors to the north. That does not count . . . "

More squinting. Then he reads directly off the paper.

" . . . 'depreciation on capital items,' which probably makes the numbers even larger."

You wonder how many people in the room know what "depreciation on capital items" means. You wonder if *you* do!

You see eyes drifting from Divertus to Lookus, who clearly is not hating the attention.

Divertus lets his hand drop and then frowns.

"Now, I could go on about the details of the library's budget and—what is perhaps much more relevant—the city's budget."

With his left hand, Lookus raises a thick, dog-eared document.

"Lookus has done an analysis of tax rates, which I, frankly, don't entirely understand, but which looks very troubling."

Lookus nods gravely. You close your eyes and count to ten.

Divertus continues. "But the point should be clear. The important problem is that we need money in the general budget *much* more than upgraded computers. And that's what we should be discussing this evening."

The man next to Lookus starts talking with him. You can't hear what the man is saying except two words: "thirty percent!" Then the man's eyes open wide. Your own eyes drift over to the dog-eared document Divertus is now holding. It can't be less than fifty pages. Maybe much more. Someone in the front row is shaking his head and saying something about taxes.

Over the years, you have gotten used to Lookus falling into his I've-got-the-highest-IQ-in-the-room game and Divertus's sending meetings off into outer space. Both men are harmless, really, but can be very annoying when they blunder into something you care about. A part of you would like to shove something back in their faces—you know details about the proposal that they cannot. You ought to be able to use that to your advantage. But one of Hank's principles was to resist that temptation. Many times last night he said, "Always treat people with respect."

Hank looks at his notes. You take a deep breath and try to focus, which, you find once again, is not easy.

Okay. The question of whether you can afford an idea is obviously legitimate. But that's not where Divertus is going. He seems to be trying to turn this into some kind of budget summit.

Any discussion that dips into budgets, especially if the topic veered off into the city's budget, could go on forever (more death by delay?). It could be filled with all sorts of unanswerable questions and misinformation, so the crowd becomes perplexed (more confusion). The audience could also get sucked into arguing about emotional subjects like tax rates (fear mongering), while the clock keeps ticking away. You realize that something must be said to salvage the discussion, but you can't quite figure out what would work.

Hank says, "I agree that more money would be useful, Divertus. But this conversation isn't about the library's total budget. Or the city's. The conversation tonight is about our library's computers, the problems with them, a proposal of how to upgrade them at a bargain price, and the benefit to the town, the library, and the library's users. Maybe at a later date, we might look at the city's budget and how much is allocated to the library."

You can see by the expression on Divertus's face that he is not ready to back down, especially with Lookus feeding him more slips of paper.

"I grant you," Hank continues, "that money is always an issue for most of us. But I really would be surprised if successful organizations—libraries, businesses, hospitals, whatever—are created by budgets that everyone thinks are adequate."

You watch the audience.

"From what I've seen," Hank says, "good organizations are much more likely to be created by dedicated people, like the library staff and those individuals who put in time to help create this proposal. They are created by the efficient use of scarce resources. And they are undoubtedly created by good ideas—such as the one under review now."

Divertus opens his mouth while looking at the latest sheets of paper provided by Lookus. When Divertus sees the two women sitting on either side of him nodding, he hesitates.

Hank looks left, then right.

Before Divertus can say more, four hands go up.

You start to say something, but stop. It's useful to try to remember, Hank had said, that although folks like Divertus and Lookus can be troublemakers, they aren't bad people. Divertus is not dodging taxes, dumping trash on the public streets, or plotting to overthrow the federal government. At least, probably not. So don't treat him as if he were.

You bite your tongue.

Despite those four hands in the air and without a pause in the interaction, someone stands up without raising his hand first.

Oh joy. It's Pompus Meani time.

POMPUS IS ACTUALLY WEARING A VEST. He puffs up his chest and says, "This proposal is, in a way, very clever, and I would have to congratulate you for preparing it."

Your patience with Pompous has sunk lower and lower over the years. You wish someone would say, "Sit down!" Unfortunately, there is little chance of that.

"But in all honesty and candor," Pompus continues, "I would have to say that you are surely exaggerating here. I believe, if you look at the *big* picture, securing a few computers for our library is not an issue of any significance. Now let me be clear, I am not suggesting that money in the library budget is the issue, either. Surely, we should be focusing on the master plan for the town. That affects all of us, young and old, rich and poor—many more people than use the library."

For some reason, hard to pinpoint, he actually looks statesmanlike.

"Of course, dealing with the master plan will require a person of broad vision, but I'm sure you can find him."

One of your neighbors rolls his eyes.

"We all understand that one must make choices. This computer issue, I would have to say, is an extremely low priority. I don't wish to be unduly critical, really I don't"—your neighbor coughs, probably to stifle a giggle—"especially since you have no doubt worked hard on this. But I must say, in all candor, that I fear you have wasted your time."

So he compliments you, is gracious, then, although he "hates to have to do it," pulls a lemon meringue pie and throws it at Hank's face (talk about ridicule!).

Jane Gallager, who is sitting next to you, is no doubt livid, since she has spent many, many hours working on this project. You turn ever so slightly and you can see that Jane is beet red. She opens her mouth, but before words come out, you grab her hand—firmly. She stares at you semi-defiantly, but manages to keep her lips zipped.

You turn your head back and see some people nodding. It is amazing, really, that anyone listens to this man who constantly broadcasts his importance ("will require a person of broad vision," like him!) and who, in the most gentlemanly way, pounds on others (like you, Hank, and Jane). But some people do listen because, what . . . He is articulate? Intelligent? Has an air of authority? Is intimidating?

Your mind tries to generate and evaluate response options as the clock ticks away. Pompus looks ever so concerned about the future of every man, woman, and child in the city. The audience is waiting. And your friends sit on their hands!

Hank clears his throat and says, "I would respectfully disagree, Pompus."

And although it is difficult for you to imagine how anyone could say "respectfully" with a straight face, Hank somehow does.

"I've been at the library and seen some of our children wasting their time with the current inadequate computers. The pressure that is on these kids—well, it certainly is much more than when I was their age."

That's clearly true.

Hank continues. "Some of them seem to work fourteen hours a day with school and homework and, in some cases, part-time jobs. From their point of view, or at least for many of them, this is hardly a problem we have exaggerated."

You turn your head and look at Melinda, the poster child for the overworked and less-than-affluent high school student. Hank turns, too. Seeming embarrassed by the eyes on her, she nevertheless pulls a book bag from underneath the table and puts it top on the table. The bag looks as if it were manufactured shortly after World War II and weighs a hundred pounds.

Hank says nothing. Finally, Pompus breaks the silence and says, graciously, "I think you overstate, but, yes, we must always take care of the children. Without question."

He looks even more statesmanlike as he sits in a sort of regal manner, seemingly as if he thinks the score is Pompus 1, Hank and You, 0.

You pick up a plastic bottle sitting on the table in front of you and take a sip of water.

TWO HANDS SHOOT UP. AS YOU look at them and the rest of the audience, too, it appears that Hank's responses so far certainly haven't created any problems, and you see a few more people nodding their heads now than twenty minutes ago. It occurs to you that if Hank stopped right now and there were a vote, you might get a 51 percent approval from generally thoughtful, rational people. But you remember once again that a coolly logical 51 percent vote, as Hank said a number of times last night, is not what you need.

He said that 51 percent may win a presidential election (or not), but here you need a lot more people *feeling* (not just thinking) that the idea is *important* (not just logical). Otherwise, when the proposal runs into some problems as it is being implemented—and there are always some problems caused by uncertainties or the naysayers—it might still be derailed because not enough people pitch in with the time and energy required to solve those problems. And that is obviously an unacceptable outcome.

ALLIS WELLI IS ONE OF THE two people waving hands at Hank, but Allis is doing so almost frantically. She obviously is not giving up yet. Hank nods in her direction.

Her voice is no longer the least bit friendly: "If this is an issue of significance, and if the library staff has not already solved the problem, then aren't you really saying that the staff is not doing its job? I think that is unwarranted, unsupported by any facts, and, frankly, *insulting*."

Any people drifting off to sleep instantly become alert. Sparks certainly catch people's attention!

Hank nods gently and stares off into space. Then he says, "If I have in any way suggested that I think the staff is doing a poor job, then I apologize, Allis. The issue certainly is not about competence or incompetence.

"The issue here is how we can equip the people on the library staff to do their work at the highest standard possible—which is what they, and you, certainly want."

You nod. It's obviously true.

"We see a problem that is stopping our staff from offering the sort of services that we need, and we have found a way with this proposal that will help solve the problem. We give our staff better tools—in this case, better computers. For all the work they do for us, they deserve the best tools."

He pauses as people seem to be grasping his point. It's clever, and true. The library can both have a competent staff *and* have a computer problem. It's not a matter of either-or.

You see the chief librarian, a wonderfully sweet older woman. Hank offers a respectful nod of his head. She doesn't stand up and applaud, but she does smile.

You are still perspiring, but much less so than five minutes ago.

THE NEXT QUESTION COMES FROM SOMEONE in the back of the room. You can't see who it is.

"Hank, I assume that all the full-time library staff are behind this?"

Hank turns his head to Jane, who clears her throat and says in about as loud a voice as she can, "Completely."

The chief librarian stands, slowly, turns to face the person who asked the question, and says yes.

The man in the back of the room says, "Thanks. Then I, for one, think this is a good idea."

It occurs to you that you might offer this person, whoever he is, a gift certificate or something. But there immediately is a next question, this time from none other than Nici Oldman.

NICI MUST BE IN HIS MID-EIGHTIES. You can't remember him talking in a town meeting for years now. The possibilities tonight are many. Could he be computer illiterate and therefore not entirely comfortable with the computers? Would he genuinely prefer that any new proposals were about getting more of the types of books he likes, not all about computers? Because he is a man of very modest means, has Pompus paid him off?

Hank calls on him. He stands and speaks.

"Could we have a quick bathroom break?"

It's hard not to smile. Hank tells everyone that he thinks it's a good idea. People start to stand up. You go looking to refill your water bottle.

3.

saving the day in centerville, part two

During the break, a few people relentlessly give you advice, much of it contradictory. One person walks by, self-consciously avoiding looking you in the eyes. But, thank goodness for small gifts, at least three or four people smile broadly, give you a thumbs-up, or in some other way signal that things might actually be going very well.

Much flows through your mind at light speed. Hank talked last night about the power of confusion and death by delay and how this means that less can often be more, in responding to veiled attacks. That is clearly what he is doing in his own responses, and it is working. Isn't it? But why aren't more people who clearly favor the proposal speaking up? Do they assume they have enough votes locked up already or that Hank is doing such a good job he doesn't need them?

As you start walking back to the front of the room, Seth, a psychiatrist, tells you that Hank is handling the fight-or-flight problem exceptionally well. You vaguely know what he is referring to: controlling the instinct to start a brawl or just bug out. Seth clearly finds this a fascinating topic to discuss now. You don't.

In less than fifteen minutes, your fellow townsfolk are more or less back in their seats.

Your self-confidence has grown. You nevertheless wish that the vote was immediate and strongly positive and that you could go home.

But, of course, that's a wish, not reality.

Avoidus Riski waves her hand in Hank's face.

AVOIDUS IS A SALESPERSON AT A local bookstore, where she is generally kind and helpful and can be pretty sharp. Unfortunately, she has not enjoyed a great deal of personal success, due to some bad breaks and some regrettable decisions she made after graduating from college. Now, she seems often to be a fearful person, although she hides this feeling. From last night's conversation with Hank, you anticipated that she might be at the meeting tonight and that her fears might focus on your plan.

"Maybe we do have an opportunity here," Avoidus says, "but I don't see how your plan addresses any number of issues that could create problems for us."

Her left hand rises into view and up pops her index finger signaling number one.

"What about the definition of a 'Centerville family'? Your proposal says that one computer will be given to the library free for every six families that purchase a computer. But what is a 'Centerville family'? Just a husband and wife? Are their grown children included? What about a sister-in-law? And who decides this? Lawyers could come at us from the computer store if the definition is too broad and, perhaps, even from citizens if our definition is too narrow."

The word *lawyers* turns a few pleasant or neutral expressions in the meeting room into frowns. Your mind drifts to Hank's phrase *fear mongering*.

"What about the possibility of Centerville Computers' jacking up prices? Have you calculated the possible markups and their impact on the proposal? Did anyone do a spreadsheet?"

You blink twice when she says the word "spreadsheet" with a perfectly serious look on her face.

"What about assuring that the computers aren't factory rejects? Do you have a process to check each machine that comes in? And who would do the checking? And when? And at what cost? And what about hidden costs down the road?"

It is beginning to sound as if you are proposing to force Grandmother Frank to go bungee jumping.

You vaguely remember that last night, Hank called this the "what about, what about, what about" attack. He also said that it is often handled poorly. People can what-if you forever, and even if you try patiently to answer what can be unanswerable questions, the impression can grow that there are an endless number of uncertainties, which in turn increases the perceived risk, possibly to an unacceptable level.

Gently, Hank says, "Avoidus, if I might cut in . . . "

With some reluctance, she does cease sharing with everyone her seemingly endless list.

"You're correct, Avoidus, we have not yet had time to look at all the many details. Nor do we have time now, since for this proposal to move forward, we need to approve the basic plan tonight. But I am sure that all your concerns will be addressed in due course."

He pauses to look at his notes.

"I admit, I can't offer a hundred percent proof of that right now. But I hope we keep in mind that attractive and innovative opportunities that can help people don't come along every day. And don't good new ideas always raise more questions than can practically be answered at first? As we move forward, the details must be handled well, there is no question there. And I hope you will help us with that."

Avoidus looks around the room, you suspect, searching for support. Not wanting to stick her neck out much—she is a risk avoider—when she sees little to no enthusiasm for her comments, she says no more.

SOMEONE ON THE LEFT SIDE OF the room raises his hand. You do not know him. Hank points his way, and the man says, "Avoidus makes a good point, and I for one have heard enough. What do you do in a meeting like this when you want a show of hands? Call the question, or something?"

The man is frowning and not at all talking in a friendly voice. The two people on either side of him look equally grumpy. Why? Do they just want to get home? Like Allis Welli and Avoidus, are they unhappy with the proposal? And do they think a quick vote now, after a series of negative remarks, might produce 51 percent of the vote against the proposal? You are trying to read their expressions more closely when Bendi Windi's hand pops up.

RIGHT BEFORE THE MEETING, BENDI HAD told you she thought the proposal was a "wonderful, wonderful" idea. She went on and on until you had to politely cut her off so you could review your speaking notes.

This could be good. She will praise the proposal perhaps just when it needs strong praise.

Bendi is a kind and dedicated schoolteacher—bubbly, fun, likes to talk, pleasant to listen to, but a little quirky. Unfortunately—unlike an hour ago—she is no longer smiling.

"You seem to have answers to everything," she tells Hank. "But what I hear worries me. You're talking about putting a lot of effort into upgrading technology, yet shouldn't we really be concentrating on improving our collections? We're all about books, reading, literacy, and learning . . . Correct?"

She looks around the room, as if to make sure she is saying what others already think.

"That's what we care about. That is what we have *always* cared about. And I for one cannot believe there is no relationship between our values and the success of this library." She pauses, looking a bit anxious to see if anyone will challenge what seems unchallengeable. "But think for a moment about this plan. Is it about collections and books? Is it—at its very core—about reading and literacy? I don't see how. It seems to me that this plan *undermines* our traditional values."

Blam. She sits. You should have seen it coming. The majority of strongly worded comments tonight have been negative. And although Hank's responses have been excellent, Bendi tends to go with the crowd.

Your mind spins. What is she saying? Allis said something like this already. Didn't she? But the focus here is on "undermining traditional values" not on "we've been successful—why risk a change?"

There is a piece of you that wants Hank to wave this away and get on with it. Over the years, you have heard too many good ideas subjected to the traditional-values attack by people who couldn't care less about traditional values, people who either have another agenda or are sincere but want to live in a mythical past.

But you also know there is a valid issue here, and you immediately think of Chapman's hardware store just down the road from the library. Some other people will be thinking the same—and this makes you nervous.

Mike Chapman's father built the town's biggest hardware store with an almost obsessive belief that every single customer should be treated well. But when Mike's dad died and Mike took over, this value began to disappear. Long-service employees retired. Times changed. New hires were in a new generation, growing up under different circumstances. Mike seems to have done nothing in response. You know he doesn't give his new people any training in handling customers because your neighbor's son worked there last summer. The consequences are clear.

It's a different business today, not just in the products the store sells but much more importantly in what the employees deeply care about. You doubt if anyone in Centerville is happy about that.

Hank is nodding his head again. "Actually, Bendi, I wonder if the surest way to abandon traditional values would be to fail to change as times change. I'm sure history is filled with examples of organizations and nations that lost what they valued most because they failed to adapt."

You watch the audience, not just Bendi.

"I certainly agree with you that our library has served the town well over the years because the staff cared so much about literacy and learning. It's hard for me to imagine why we would want to change that. But if we don't give our people the latest tools that can help the institution truly stand for literacy and learning, we'll be selling the future of our city short. Over time, people in the town would notice the lack of tools and deteriorating staff and stop using our library. And so, what we have traditionally valued would gradually disappear."

He pauses, seemingly to catch his breath.

"Anyway, I think what we need is in our proposal—to help the library *uphold* something that is so important and that it has always stood for. I suppose that sounds a bit convoluted—we have to change in some ways in order to remain the same in other ways. But I can think of many examples of where traditional values were lost because people didn't change with the times."

He doesn't say "like Mike Chapman's hardware store," but you notice a few people glancing over at one of Mike's retired employees. He is giving Hank a look that seems to say, You've got that right. It's a shame Mike's son didn't.

BEFORE BENDI CAN MAKE ANY COMEBACK, Lookus Smarti stands and says, "It seems to me your plan is too *simplistic*."

He makes "simplistic" sound more like "moronic."

"A few computers are being proposed as a silver bullet to solve the complex challenges you yourself admitted libraries have these days."

Neither you nor Hank said anything about a silver bullet.

"I agree that good computers in the library would be convenient," Lookus says, "but does this even matter when most people have their own computers at home these days?"

Poor kids don't. Neither do some of the older people on fixed incomes.

Lookus continues. "The real key to excellence in a library is complex. It involves the quality of the librarians, their pay and benefits packages, the quality of the books, the use of limited space, the maintenance on the building—well, I could go on and on."

You wish he wouldn't. Of course, he does.

"You don't seem to understand that. It's absurd to suggest that a few new computers are some sort of magical, zirconium bullet."

Lookus sits, looking smug. Your mind wanders for a second. Is there a metal called zirconium?

You try to concentrate. What is he saying? One simple plan will not single-handedly cure all ills. True, and no one behind this idea has ever suggested you are trying to solve all problems with the computer proposal.

Hank says, "Lookus, if we have presented this idea in a way that sounds as if the new computers will take care of the library's many challenges, then we presented it poorly. Excellence requires quality books, efficient use of space, good but inexpensive maintenance, and, most of all, great staff."

Last night, Hank told you a memorable story about one irritating man in his company who often shoots down ideas by saying they are "hopelessly simplistic," given the complexity of some problem. Hank also shared with you the most effective way he had seen for dealing with that sort of attack.

"Lookus, the library staff has asked for help with the specific problem of the computers, and that's why we are discussing it. They know, and we know, it's only one piece of a much bigger picture, but a piece where we were fortunate enough to find a great opportunity to make a contribution."

Hank smiles softly. "So—no magic zirconium bullet here. That would, indeed, be an unrealistically simplistic solution. The proposal is just one piece of a much bigger picture, the center of which is always good people doing what we need them to do and what they themselves believe in."

The head librarian is now broadly smiling.

Your brain is, once again, moving at near light speed. Smiling librarian = good. An unending series of grenades sent your way = bad. Hank's handling of the situation = superb so far. Pompus looking alert and crafty in the third row = exceptionally annoying.

Hank is doing no more than what he described to you last night. Yet you are still amazed at how well he is dispatching the zingers using his basic formula of respecting everyone, keeping his answers simple and sensible, constantly watching the entire audience, and (apparently) using the detail in his 3 pages of notes. You glance at the table in front of Hank. Just 3 pages, not 33 (or 133)!

You notice a neighbor in the first row staring at you. He has been having a very tough time. After being laid off two years ago, for fourteen months he passed job offers below his skill level until he found a good position. Tragically, that company then ran into an economic stone wall and he was out of a job again. Tonight, he looks beaten. He has two kids and little chance of a home computer that is better than the inadequate ones currently at the library. It's sad. And unjust.

YOU COULD USE ANOTHER FRIENDLY COMMENT from the audience. But the only hand up is from . . . Avoidus Riski. Hank calls on her.

"I'm worried," she tells the audience, "because no one else does this. Do they? I mean, if this was such a great idea, why hasn't it been done already?"

The man to her right makes that sort of expression with his face that we associate with, "I hadn't thought of that."

Avoidus continues. "My guess is that as we move along, Centerville Computers will come to realize this is just not a good marketing investment and the whole deal will fall apart."

She sits.

Hank says, "Avoidus, I agree this is a first in Centerville. But, as they say, there is a first time for everything. I know similar arrangements must have been made in some other towns, although, I grant you, not exactly like ours."

You focus. What may have changed recently that would make this sort of deal more practical or advantageous today than in the past? Hank is clearly on the same wavelength, since he says, "I recently read that the tax treatment for such 'promotional' donations has just changed, making it more favorable for companies. That may be one reason that other cities have not previously done this."

You try to think of a better example to add to Hank's. Nothing occurs to you. But maybe it doesn't matter.

"And generally," he continues, "organizations like our library *do* have to get more creative these days because so much does seem to change. Overall, I think it's great that we might be at the leading edge of something."

It occurs to you that *you* thought of how Hank would answer *before* he did so. That makes you feel good (and your anger goes down a notch). You're learning.

TWO MORE PEOPLE SPEAK UP TO endorse the proposal. We'll skip the details since all they really say is, This is obviously a good idea; we should vote yes now.

But then . . .

Pompus smiles his good-natured smile and once again stands up. He looks toward Hank but ever-so-slightly avoids eye contact with him. "I do appreciate the effort a number of you have expended on this, and your answers to my earlier concerns have been comforting. But, I fear that there is still a fatal flaw in your plan, of which you seem to be unaware."

He has something in his hand.

"I have here a newspaper article, from last year, concerning a house fire which was caused by a malfunctioning computer. The computer in question was purchased from ... Centerville Computers."

He looks highly concerned and oh-so-caring about his neighbors.

"It's clear you were unaware of this problem, or in the interests of full disclosure, you would have mentioned it by now. This is worrisome because I wonder what other issues may have been overlooked in the haste with which this plan has been formed. Under the circumstances, I think we would be well served if this proposal is referred to the library safety committee in order to ensure that we will not be exposing the facility to any unwarranted risk."

You know nothing of that fire, but Pompus must have known for some time. He could have alerted you in advance so you could have checked to see if there was any real issue here. But he chose to try to embarrass you publicly with a gotcha, all the while offering a gracious, statesmanlike smile.

A few people in the audience do suddenly look concerned, but more of them look annoyed. Are they getting tired of Pompus's antics?

Your mind moves like a racecar (you're getting better at this). Hank (or you) could respond to this latest attack by saying that one instance proves nothing (which is true). But Pompus would then have you on the defensive and could say something like, "Well, yes, that is obviously true, but imagine a fire, it grows out of control, someone is hurt. What if the someone were a child or Miss Henley?" Miss Henley is one of two assistant librarians. She is sweet and grandmotherly and very popular. So then you say ... what? The probability of such an event is low? The hospital is not that far away?

Hank says, "First of all, thank you for your kind words about appreciating my effort, but I must emphasize they don't apply just to me—a large team has developed this plan. Thanks, everyone."

Hank's response is clever. So, Pompus, you are attacking a whole team of people whom you suggest are all killers of children and nice elderly women.

"And thanks, Pompus, the fire you mention is also helpful to hear about—we are still on the lookout for things to double-check as we move ahead."

Ha! *You* chime in for the first time: "Actually, that's why we sent out the plan in advance of the meeting, so we could check out any such concerns beforehand. Previously no one, not even the fire chief, has expressed any safety concern about the offer from Centerville Computers, but now we will certainly look into it as you suggest."

The fire chief is respected in the town. You continue: "I *can* say, though, that numerous other potential concerns have been brought up in advance and all have been easily addressed. I'll bet the same will be true in this case—after all, these are standard safety-approved, name-brand computers. I really don't think we need to ask our safety committee to review the work of Underwriters Laboratories. But, of course, we *will* look into this."

And just in case there are other such credibility-challenging gotchas lurking in the audience, you quickly add, "And if anyone else has not had a chance to tell us about anything that might sound like a serious problem, just let one of us know after the meeting tonight or tomorrow. We will check it out immediately. If there is a problem, I'm confident someone will find a creative solution—which is what has happened with every single potential issue we have encountered so far."

You worry for a second that what you said may have been too rat-a-tat and not appropriately respectful. But Hank nods reassuringly. And adds nothing.

Maybe you are getting the hang of this.

DIVERTUS ATTENTI JUMPS UP AND SAYS, "These seats certainly are hard." He smiles. "I, for one, would appreciate another break. Maybe twenty or, better yet, twenty-five minutes this time. I know a group of us could use this opportunity to talk about another proposal facing the City Council."

You see where this can go and speak up without even looking at Hank.

"I think people want to get home soon, so let's stick to the whole point of this meeting."

You see a few people squirming in their (hard, wooden) seats.

"But maybe a five-minute stretch-our-legs break is a good idea."

Hank nods, Divertus frowns, and people start to stand up.

WHILE THE MEETING IS IN RECESS, you grab Hank and duck out the rear entrance of the hall to get away from the swarm of well-wishers, distracters, and advice givers who will no doubt try to descend upon you.

"You're doing great," you tell Hank. "But when are they going to give up?"

He shrugs. "First of all, *we're* doing well. It's not just me anymore. And keep in mind that 'they' are only about ten percent of the crowd. You are right, though; they are being persistent."

Hank looks at the notes he has in his left hand and says, with remarkable calm, "There are a lot more ways that people could pull this off track."

You look at Hank's notes. You see his cryptic handwriting, describing attack after attack:

- This puts us on a slippery slope!

- It doesn't go far enough.

- It goes too far!

- You can't have it both ways! First you said . . .

- It's just too much work, and we are already over-loaded.

- You'll never convince enough people.

- We're not equipped to do this. We don't have ...

Hank sees your expression and says, "Yes, these can be disruptive. But there are simple, honest responses to all of these concerns, too."

You hear a noise. Someone is coming, and a voice calls out, "Hank, are you out here? We're ready to start again."

4.

saving the day in centerville, part three

When you walk back in the door, you catch sight of a woman whose teenage daughter you met twice while working on the library proposal. You don't know the mother, but you know she's having a tough time. Divorced? Unemployed? Health problems without much insurance? The chances are very slim that the girl has easy access to a top-quality computer and printer with high-speed Internet access.

You clap your hands and people in the room stop shuffling.

The chair says, "Well, then let's continue."

Lookus Smarti is on his feet immediately. "As I have been listening to the conversation, it now occurs to me that we have really tried this sort of arrangement before and it didn't work. I'm surprised I didn't think of it earlier."

You have no idea what he might be referring to.

"Six years ago: I refer to the plumbing store and the fire department."

He pauses, looking smug that he has been able to come up with this piece of obscure history.

"The fire department budget was under great pressure. They absolutely required," he blinks and stares off into space, "about four percent more money than was available. Calvin's Plumbing Supplies offered to replace their old pipes in a promotional arrangement much like this one. And do you remember what happened?"

Most people in the audience look a bit perplexed—but nevertheless interested.

"Not enough people took part in the store's offer, the fire department got ahead of itself assuming the arrangement would work, some demolition was done, adequate supplies did not come, and it was a mess."

Lookus proceeds to go into some gruesome detail about pipes and tolerances and what happened in a restroom. It's basically another fear-mongering tactic. Remember the Bomb. This is the same thing, he's saying, possibly a different color, but still an exploding device. So keep it out of town.

You think you've talked about this very tactic last night. A good response, Hank said, is neither "That's ridiculous," at one extreme, nor a mind-numbing and time-consuming attempt to examine some incident in the past, where you could easily not have enough information to put up a good response and thus end up looking as if you haven't done your homework. A good response, he said, is simply, "That was then; this is now. The first group that tried to build a PC failed and probably looked pretty silly, but that didn't make it a bad idea forever."

Now Hank quickly offers an example even better than PCs: "The person who tried to manufacture a car that anyone could afford failed in his first attempt and had to lay off people and suffer through financial difficulties. Thank goodness, that *did not* stop Henry Ford." When many heads nod, Hank immediately moves on.

Hank points to Heidi Agenda before Lookus can make a comeback.

"It just occurred to me that the timing for this idea may be wrong," she says. "Isn't the library in its peak purchasing season? Doesn't that require a great deal of concentrated attention from the staff? Wouldn't this make more sense in two or three months?"

In your opening remarks, you said very clearly that if you don't move ahead tonight, the offer is dead. Heidi is not an idiot. Therefore, once again, she must be . . .

You wonder what she is really concerned about. It occurs to you, uncharitably, that a powerful truth serum might be required to extract the truth from her, assuming she even understands her own true agenda. It also occurs to you that this is a useless train of thought.

More usefully, you realize that you have seen the wrong-timing argument used many times in your life. "We must wait for another project to finish before we start a new one." "The city has a major initiative with fire trucks. We cannot handle a second initiative now.

We'll have to wait until the first has been finished." It's more death by delay.

Hank acknowledges that we should always be on the lookout for overload. But on the other hand . . . "Maybe it's useful to remember that we *can* walk and chew gum at the same time. At least I think I can."

A few people chuckle.

Remembering last night's tutorial, you add, "From what I've seen over the years, projects don't have to be one hundred percent done before another can be successfully started. They can overlap. Often it isn't even clear when you would mark the start of one initiative and the end of another."

Hank acknowledges that it is, of course, possible that you might have 122 projects and that adding number 123 would be silly. But if that were the case, which it is not here, you wouldn't even propose a new idea before raising an even better one: cut the 122 down to something manageable.

As Hank is wrapping up his response, you recall a case at work when a perfectly intelligent colleague tried to shoot down a good plan by saying, "This excellent idea would better synergize with the firm's fiftieth anniversary," which was ten years away.

HEIDI DOES NOT SIT DOWN. She is not giving up.

"Those are good points," she acknowledges.

The volume of her voice and her apparent conviction is growing. You notice that a group of people on the left who were probably text-messaging their spouses, children, barbers—who knows—have stopped and are now listening.

"Okay, look, maybe this is a good plan, but it's not going to work *here*." Heidi shakes her head sternly for emphasis. "I know in big cities this sort of wheeling and dealing with merchandise like computers goes on a lot, but I also know that big city libraries are often run-down, unfriendly places. Our library is a warm, personal place, and I'm not sure commercial sponsorship will fit in here at all."

It's a clever attack. It draws on a real truth: everyone *is* different. Centerville *is* different from Bigtown. I am different from you. Pompus is different from other creatures in the forest.

At work today, you actually discussed the we're-different angle with a friend (because Hank had raised it last night). She said she had heard this argument used many times in many different ways. So have you. She reminded you of Dave, a coworker who once argued that a new idea used in banking would never work in your industry. When informed that one of your competitors was using the idea, Dave retreated into something like "But that firm has a different culture from ours." When it was pointed out that your own Dallas office had adopted the idea, Dave, in a rather desperate last stand, said that Texas was *different*.

Hank says, "Heidi, you are correct that we are not like a really big town, and we all want to keep Centerville as cozy, safe, and clean as possible. But that doesn't mean we can't learn some valuable lessons from other places. After all, people are basically the same everywhere. And when you compare most things between a big city or medium sized or small, you find more similarities than differences. We go to work, we shop, we raise children, we watch TV . . ."

Heidi comes back at Hank, restating her initial position. But as it becomes clear she has no new angle and few people seem interested in listening to her anymore, she hesitates, then stops.

YOU ARE BEGINNING TO THINK THAT maybe the proposal cannot be derailed at this point. Hank deftly handles two more attacks, and you manage one all by yourself. The number of heads that are nodding keeps going up and up. You might even have over 70 percent of the vote if you . . .

You hear someone loudly clearing her throat. It's Spaci Cadetus. She's a nice person. Most people think she commutes to work each day from her home on Jupiter.

"Your plan requires more room for computers, but the library stays the same size. Right? I mean, we're not building some new wing or anything. So we are, if you think about it, shrinking the actual library. Before you know it, you will be asking us for a coffee corner and—poof!—more of the library is gone. Eventually, we will be left with a multipurpose entertainment facility without a book in sight!"

Before Hank can open his mouth, someone from the back of the room yells, "She may have a point."

Again before Hank can speak up, one of your friends, and a supporter of the proposal, yells, "It's a stupid point. It's clear to me now that this is a great idea. I can't believe we are wasting time on this drivel."

"Drivel" leaves Spaci waving her hands. "Drivel!! Who said that?!"

Any heads that were staring at shoes or laps suddenly rise and start to look around the room. Those of your neighbors who appeared to be falling asleep quickly wake up.

"I did," says your friend Blindus Loyalus, with no intention of backing down. Lookus Smarti stands up. Almost leaps up.

"Oddly, given the source, it is not 'drivel,'" Lookus says. "It is an important point. This proposal could put us on a slippery slope, not to a building without books but—"

Your friend yells, "Will you just for once in your life *shut up!*"

Lookus is nearly speechless. He sputters, "Slippery-slope problems are very serious. It has been documented in much literature about the Vietnam war—"

Blindus is out of control. "Vietnam!!! Oh, that's a good one. We put in computers, and—"

It's a food fight.

A voice from the back yells, "Slippery-slope problems are often unrecognized and can be serious."

A moan goes up from at least two sections of the audience. Another voice comes from somewhere. "We could ask Lookus and a few others to look into the issue."

Another angry participant says, "Come on. We have to decide tonight. The last thing we need is a task force."

Spaci says, "Perhaps if we broke the room into two or three groups right now and—"

Dear Lord.

You wave your hands. "Come on, folks."

Someone off to the left says, "Spaci, would you just go . . . water your lawn or something."

Someone in the first row says to his neighbor, "This is bad."

His neighbor says, "Not really. When people care about an issue, you always get some emotion. That's just life."

This (wise) comment comes from Barry, an elementary school teacher. You say, loud enough for all to hear, "Barry, could you speak up?"

With virtually everyone now paying attention, he does, somewhat reluctantly.

"I was just saying that our breaking out into a mild yelling match is nothing to worry about, because it's just human nature. That's just the way people are."

He turns around in his seat so he is facing others.

"Sometimes we teachers do look like our ten-year-old students. But it's actually worse if there is no discussion, no objections, no emotion. That usually means people don't care, so good luck if you are going to need their help in making whatever it is happen. Or it means no one has thought about the idea, so we make a bad decision or one that benefits just a single person or group."

You couldn't have said it better. And Barry has credibility in the community.

"I'm not suggesting we continue to act as less than adults," our teacher continues, with a gentle laugh. "We need to show respect for one another."

He looks at Spaci, and she shrinks in her chair.

"But let's not get uptight if we get a little emotional. At least we're here. Almost all of us could have stayed at home tonight. And after we leave, we'll know more about what will be happening. I know I'm now ready to help if the proposal starts to run into difficulties after we approve it."

Looking left then right, you can easily see that virtually everybody in the room seems to be listening after the excitement of the food fight. You need to add nothing; nor does Hank.

Thank you, Barry.

HEIDI STANDS UP AGAIN. WHATEVER IS motivating her is obviously a pretty big deal.

"Look, I don't question the possible value of what you are proposing. If my prior comments suggested that, you misinterpret me. My concerns are very practical. For example, I think you are kidding yourselves if you believe Centerville Computers is going to cover *all* our costs."

"Kidding yourselves" is more ridicule, another attack on the competence of you, Jane, Hank, and others. You notice a person in the second row nodding wisely, which, of course, is irritating at this point in the meeting. But most people seem to be rolling their eyes or smiling at you.

Heidi continues. "What about the inevitable upgrades and maintenance—who is going to pay that bill? And what will we have to sacrifice when we get stuck with it? So although your proposal seems like a good idea on the surface"—she did say it was a bad idea earlier in the meeting—"we need more money to make it work. Where will the money come from?"

You quickly see it's yet another form of fear mongering, but this time, it's less about the proposal than the aftertaste. It's like the situation where everyone agrees to buy a German shepherd to guard the firehouse at night, but then it's discovered that feeding the dog will destroy the city budget. So a big guard dog is basically a good idea, but it can't be made to happen in a practical way.

Hank says, "You are certainly right on one point, Heidi. These computers will need support, just as all computers do."

You think to yourself that Hank will probably say that it would serve no useful purpose to list all maintenance issues and talk about each. And, indeed . . .

"But that doesn't mean," Hank says, "we can't afford them. As I said—or at least meant to say—I have been told that Jane and others have calculated the maintenance costs down to the penny. And even if the calculations are a bit low, why can't we find efficiencies elsewhere? Just the other day, for example, the power company was telling me about all sorts of ways to reduce our power bill, and there are probably a number of other areas where we could save money if we put our minds to it. And why wouldn't we put our minds to it?"

You suspect that the people working in the library have always stayed within their budget, so the argument is sound. Looking around the room as Heidi talked and Hank responded—you have by now developed the habit of constantly watching the audience—you see no evidence that people haven't bought Hank's response.

What you also see is that at least three or four small groups of people, scattered throughout the audience, have been having conversations the entire time Heidi was talking, and not with whispers. One group of three people, sitting in the first row, is highly animated with nods and hand movements and fast speech. Instead of listening to Heidi, they seem to be talking about implementing the proposal.

It dawns on you that the conversation has gone from "We need no proposal, because there is no problem" to "Okay, there is a problem, but your proposal to deal with it is flawed" to "Okay, we have a problem and the proposal is good, but we'll never be able to make the good idea work here." Or something close to that. And now, people are running out of excuses for why it won't work here.

THERE IS A MOMENT OF SILENCE in the room. Someone in the back sticks up his hand, but just as quickly pulls it down. The chair notes that there seem to be no further questions, and he calls for a vote. Before he can call for a show of hands, someone in the middle of the room shouts out, "Come on, folks. I came in here not entirely sure what this was all about. But now it is obvious that this is a great idea. It deserves our support." After a very brief pause, he adds, "No, actually, it deserves our *enthusiastic* support."

Dozens of voices in the crowd can be heard to say "yes," "hear, hear," or "I agree." When the noise drops, the chair says, "All those in favor?"

Hands go up. With only a quick glance, it's obvious at least 80 percent have bought into the proposal, and close to half of them raised their hands quickly, with no hesitation.

"Against?"

Maybe 10 percent of those present raise their hands. Some people don't vote.

A smattering of applause breaks out and then grows louder. Some people pick up their coats and immediately head toward the doors. Most just stand or remain sitting while talking to people near them. Four of your friends walk toward you with big smiles on their faces.

Each congratulates you for a job very well done. One says something like "This is a terrific idea we just voted on, and ..." Another is saying, "Thanks for hanging in there ... " It's hard to hear clearly with all the conversations occurring simultaneously in the room.

You feel a tap on your shoulder, turn, and see Jane. She worked so hard on this proposal, and here she is, with thankful tears in her eyes.

It becomes more confusing at this point. Hank has three or four people around him, Jane is quietly talking to someone, and a few more people seem to be just watching the front of the hall where you and Hank and Jane are standing. A friend yells out, "Great job!" as he waves at you while walking out the door. You hear a group of four or five people talk energetically, with one of them saying, " ... and if we need it, *I'll* lead the effort to get even more computers ... "

Others, who were so quiet in the meeting, now seem to be talking about how one objection raised earlier was silly and how another was a really cheap shot. Where were these people a half hour ago?!

Within twenty minutes, the hall is nearly empty. Hank, too, has left (after a big apology that he had just received a call from someone about something). A few people continue to talk to Jane about what needs to happen by when and about how they might help out. You move off to the side, pack up, and quietly leave.

While heading home, you find yourself happy, of course, that the meeting is over and that the proposal was supported so well. You also find some lingering annoyance at Avoidus, Heidi, Lookus, and the like. But you wonder if, in an odd way, their presence may actually have helped.

Even your friends who supported the idea before the meeting left looking more committed to helping, if needed, and even more enthusiastic than before. Would that have happened if you made your speech, called for a quick vote, won with 55 percent, and left the hall?

You know this evening did not solve the state's budget deficit or fix the overcrowded emergency room at Biggertown Hospital. No cure for some horrible disease tonight. But nevertheless you do feel a certain pride.

You were thrown into a difficult situation. A simple, imaginative, useful idea was slammed again and again with misinformed, unfair, and outrageous concerns and questions, any of which could have wounded or killed it—despite the fact that the proposal made so much sense. And yet your team prevailed.

Because you were able to get buy-in, the library won, the town won, and kids will get the help they need. And although you haven't had time yet to sort it out in your mind, you sense that you learned any number of lessons that will serve you well in the future.

Not a bad night's work.

— The End —

the
method

part two

5.

four ways to kill a good idea

IRST OF ALL, congratulations. You handled the computer proposal very nicely. Don't be modest and give all the credit to Hank. Remember, you found him. And during the meeting, you grew enough in your understanding and capability that you became a valuable asset. You're on your way to building, or improving, a very important skill that can serve you in many ways.

Now it's time to examine more systematically what happened during that evening. What did the audience do? What did Hank do? What did you do? What exactly was your method for dealing with the attacks? Why did it succeed? Then we'll show you how to use that method the next time you need buy-in for your own good idea, or to keep someone else's good idea from being wounded or shot down.

First, let's look at the audience. A small number of people, less than a dozen in the group of seventy-five, raised concerns, questions, and arguments of the sort that can undermine buy-in for any good idea—no matter how worthy or sensible it is. Here we speak of a maddeningly effective set of attacks that can quickly destroy proposals or plans—even though you're sure the proposal, if examined carefully by an informed and impartial jury, would be embraced by a vote of twelve to zero.

We have found over two dozen of these sorts of questions and concerns that are very commonly used in a wide variety of settings. We showed many of these attacks in the library story. We'll give you a list of twenty-four later in the book. There are more than two dozen, but the twenty-four cover a lot of ground. All are potentially dangerous because they can be devilishly difficult to deal with well and because just one attack, handled poorly, can derail a discussion.

Twenty-four is a large number to memorize. But that turns out not to be necessary, because these common attacks are based on only one or more of four strategies that we have found people to employ. Anyone can easily remember the four—which can take you a long way toward dealing with them.

fear mongering

This kind of attack strategy is aimed at raising anxieties so that a thoughtful examination of a proposal is very difficult if not impossible. People begin to worry that implementing a genuinely good plan, pursuing a great idea, or making a needed vision a reality might be filled with frightening risks—even though that is not really the case.

There are all sorts of ways to create fear. You have seen a half dozen in the library story. The trick is to start with an undeniable fact and then to spin a tale that ends with consequences that are genuinely frightening or that just push the anxiety buttons we all have. The logic that goes from the fact to the dreadful consequence will be wrong, maybe even silly. A story that reminds us of scary events in the past may not be a fair analog, but it can be effective in bringing up unpleasant memories. Pushing anxiety buttons is manipulative in the worse sense of the word. But it can be an effective tactic.

Once aroused, anxieties do not necessarily disappear when a person is confronted with an analytically sound rebuttal. If humans were only logical creatures, this would not be a problem. But we are not. Far from it.

Words often play an important role in these cases. If the failure of the Amtek project led to layoffs a few years ago in your firm, then the word *Amtek* will carry meanings that can arouse very unpleasant feelings. In a more general sense, the terms *lawyers, fire,* or *big government* can stir up fear and anger in some people.

In our story, Pompus tried fear mongering with his "Aha, what about this?!" with "this" being a newspaper article about a *fire* caused by a computer sold by Centerville Computers. The whole logic of his argument was weak, if not ridiculous, but *fire* is an emotionally loaded word. Spaci Cadetus later argued that expanding the space devoted to computers puts us on *a slippery slope* that will sooner or later send us down the mountain, where the library we love would be *ruined*. Her argument about how the library would turn into an all-purpose entertainment center was preposterous, but everyone has seen slippery slopes and many of us have suffered from them. Memories of suffering can evoke fear.

We see this problem all the time when people are trying to help an organization deal with a changing environment or to exploit a new and significant opportunity. In one typical case, a sizable change was needed inside a firm. With effort, some people did develop an innovative vision of what changes would be needed and a smart strategy of how to make those changes. Then, in trying to explain this to others and achieve sufficient buy-in, the initiators ran into someone who noted (correctly) that the last time they tried a big change (in their case, the "customer centric" initiative), they were unsuccessful, and some of the consequences (impossible workloads for a while, a few good people's careers derailed) were very unpleasant. Anxiety began to grow as others used the words *customer centric* again and again. No one made a perfectly logical case for how the historical and current situations were comparable. But that didn't matter. An undercurrent of fear became a riptide, and the new change vision and strategies never gained sufficient buy-in to make the change effort successful.

Even if most people see an anxiety-creating attack for what it is, if those who don't see the fallacy of the logic constitute more than a small percentage of a group, you might still have a serious problem that must be handled with care. Even a single smart or credible person, if made fearful, can be tipped not only toward opposing a proposal, but also toward using attack tactics that tip still more people. Anxiety then builds like an infection. In this sense, the method used in the library story works like an antibiotic.

People use fear-mongering strategies with voices that are beastly or, more often, ones that are oh-so-innocently calm. People can know very clearly what they are doing and why, or they can be completely oblivious to the way they're acting. One doesn't have to be an unethical or a self-serving person to use a strategy that raises anxieties and kills off a good idea. And that fact has huge implications regarding what you must do to deal effectively with fear mongering and all the other attack strategies (more on that soon).

delay

There are questions and concerns that can kill a good proposal simply by creating a deadly delay. They so slow the communication and discussion of a plan that sufficient buy-in cannot be achieved before a critical cut-off time or date. They make what may seem like a logical suggestion but which, if accepted, will make the project miss its window of opportunity. Death-by-delay tactics can force so many meetings or so many straw polls that momentum is lost, or another idea, not nearly as good, gains a foothold.

At least a quarter of the attacks in the library story employ some sort of delay strategy. Intentionally or not, Divertus tried right at the beginning of the meeting to burn up all available time with a discussion of the library's overall budget and even the city's budget. Later, the classic let's-create-a-task-force ploy was suggested and, had it been accepted, would have so slowed the buy-in process that Centerville Computer's corporate parent would probably have withdrawn its proposal.

Death by delay can be a very powerful strategy because it's so easy to deploy. A case is made that sounds so reasonable, where we should wait (just a bit) until some other project is done, or we should send this back into committee (just to straighten up a few points), or (just) put off the activity until the next budget cycle.

With a delay strategy, attention can be diverted to some legitimate, pressing issue, the sort of which always exists. There is the sudden budget shortfall, the unexpected competitor announcement, the dangerous new bill put before the legislature, the growing problem here, the escalating conflict there. These can require immediate attention, but rarely 100 percent of people's attention. With death by delay, the point is to focus people 100 percent on the crisis so that a good idea is forgotten or crucial communication is lost. Growing momentum toward buy-in then slows to the point that it can never be regained.

We recently saw a version of this, which you might call the "we have too much on our plate right now" argument.

It is possible to have too many projects, where clearly any recommended action should be cutting back, not adding more. But in this case, the proposal was for a very innovative automotive parts product, and no one could have logically defended the superior worth of all the other projects in the works. But those who were running some of the current programs, and receiving considerable resources for doing so, correctly saw the new proposal as a threat, which they successfully killed with a too-much-on-our-plate-right-now bullet.

Because it is so easy to use, death by delay is a weapon available to nearly anyone, which makes it particularly dangerous. Yet, as with the other three attack strategies, the many little bombs it creates can all be defused.

confusion

Some idea-killing questions and concerns muddle the conversation with irrelevant facts, convoluted logic, or so many alternatives that it is impossible to have the clear and intelligent dialog that builds buy-in.

Heidi Agenda hit Hank with "what about, what about, what about?" With that attack, it's easy for a conversation to slide into endless side discussions about this and that, and that and this, and don't forget about . . . Eventually, people conclude that the idea has not been well thought out. Or they feel stupid because they cannot follow the conversation (which tends to create anger, which can flow back toward the proposal or the proposer). Or they get that head-about-to-burst feeling, which they relieve by setting aside the proposal or plan.

Some individuals can be astonishingly clever at drawing you into a discussion that is so complex that a reasonable person simply gives up and walks away. This trap was built into more than a third of the attacks in our library story. Many people used them (though a Lookus Smarti type can be exceptionally skilled at this). A confused person might still vote yes, but only to stop the conversation and with no commitment toward making the idea become a reality.

A complex topic is not needed for a confusion strategy to work. Even the simplest of plans can be pulled into a forest of complexity where nearly anyone can become lost. Statistics can be powerful weapons, used not to clarify but to bewilder. "You are trying to solve a problem that doesn't exist. Just look at this [twenty-two-page] spreadsheet. I think if we study it closely . . . " Complex stories, about which most people do not know the details, can be lethal. "What about the Teledix project [which no one has ever heard of] and the competitive strategy we have for the TX line of products [a strategy that half the people in the room know nothing of]? I worry that the interaction of Teledix, TX, and this proposal will hurt third-quarter income, at least in Asia, which would be *very* bad. Don't you think so?"

We see confusion strategies used all the time, sometimes by people who don't like a good idea, but also by a Lookus, who, perhaps unconsciously, has a need to appear to be the smartest person in the room, or by a Spaci, who just doesn't think very clearly. We recently watched a presentation communicated in PowerPoint slides, all sixty-eight of them, and many in impossible-to-read small print. Created by a Lookus, the slide deck "demonstrated" why a proposal to allocate many more resources to building a firm's business in Europe went too far. The document is incomprehensible (we have yet to find anyone in that firm who can explain it clearly), but it has successfully undermined support for a plan that is probably a very good one.

ridicule (or character assassination)

Some verbal bullets don't shoot directly at the idea but at the people behind the idea. The proposers may be made to look silly. Questions may be raised about competence. Slyly or directly, questions can be raised about character. Strong buy-in is rarely achieved if an audience feels uneasy with those presenting a proposal.

A Pompus can be exceptionally skilled at using this strategy. He raises an issue with an oh-so-innocent, yet subtly condescending look on his face. Without even saying the words, a question is raised about whether you are smart enough to have done careful homework on a problem, or visionary enough to see better alternatives.

In our meeting, we saw Bendi Windi, in her attempt to fit in with momentum going against the proposal, say that the plan abandoned the community's long cherished values, which Hank apparently must not believe in, making him of questionable character. We also saw Avoidus Riski suggest that "no one else does this," which a thoughtful proposer would surely know, raising questions about competence.

Questions and concerns based on a strategy of ridicule and character assassination can be served with a dramatic flourish of indignation, but more often are presented with a light hand. There is a sense that the attacker feels awkward even bringing up a subject, but he nevertheless feels it is his duty to ask whether George's dinners with his admin assistant might . . . No, no, that wasn't fair. Forget I said that.

The ridicule strategy is used less than the others, probably because it can snap back at the attacker. But when this strategy works, there can be collateral damage. Not only is a good idea wounded, and a person's reputation unfairly tarnished, but all the additional sensible ideas from the proposer might have less credibility, at least until the memory of the attack fades.

ATTACKS DO NOT HAVE TO BE based on only one of these strategies. The biggest bombs often draw from two or even three. So an irrational, unfair, or nasty concern tries to create confusion and a delay or builds on character assassination and fear mongering. Clever attacks based on multiple strategies can be very powerful.

Because the strategies, individually or in combination, can be so deadly, once you have been hit with them a few times you may be tempted to use them yourself when another person presents an idea that, though good, is not entirely to your liking. You are smart and skilled verbally, so you hopelessly confuse the conversation. You are sick of a meeting and want to stop it, so you try a clever fear tactic. You don't much like the presenter, so you go after his or her character. You think you don't receive enough credit and you want your ideas to "win" more often, so you send any alternative proposal into the bottomless pit of death by delay.

But the blade cuts both ways. As the library story clearly suggests, these tactics don't guarantee success and they can snap back in your face, sometimes very painfully. Ironically, it is very often pain from the past, solidified into cynicism, that can lead us to spitefully use the four attack strategies to try to stop others. We think (consciously or not) that everyone does it, so why not us. Or that the ends always justify the means. Or that nice guys finish last. Very rarely do these cynical ideas work to our advantage over time.

twenty-four attacks

The four attack strategies actually get executed using about two dozen very familiar, very generic, difficult-to-handle questions, arguments, and concerns, any of which can hurt or kill a genuinely good idea. Over time these attacks have become so common and widely used that almost anyone will recognize them. And anyone might employ them, even if he or she is not consciously trying to be unfair or nasty. They can be used nearly anywhere, regardless of the nature of the idea or the setting—making them all the more dangerous.

Here they are, listed in the order they were introduced in the Centerville story:

1. We've been successful; why change?

2. Money (or some other problem a proposal does not address) is the only real issue.

3. You exaggerate the problem.

4. You're implying that we've been failing!

5. What's the hidden agenda here?

6. What about this, and that, and this, and that . . .?

7. Your proposal goes too far/doesn't go far enough.

8. You have a chicken-and-egg problem.

9. Sounds like [something most people dislike] to me!

10. You're abandoning our core values.

11. It's too simplistic to work.

12. No one else does this.

13. You can't have it both ways.

14. Aha! You can't deny *this*! ("This" being a worrisome thing that the proposers know nothing about and the attackers keep secret until just the right moment.)

15. To generate this many questions and concerns, the idea has to be flawed.

16. We tried that before—didn't work.

17. It's too difficult to understand.

18. Good idea, but this is not the right time.

19. It's just too much work to do this.

20. It won't work here; we're different!

21. It puts us on a slippery slope.

22. We can't afford this.

23. You'll never convince enough people.

24. We're simply not equipped to do this.

We can think of a few more, and with time and a little thought, you will be able to do so, also. But these twenty-four cover most of the territory.

As we have said before, many of these questions and observations might be raised by a person who, quite honestly, is not trying to slyly sink a good idea. But that does not make any of the attacks less potentially tricky to deal with. This reality about innocent motives has powerful implications for making a response method effective.

There is a very specific way to deal with each of the twenty-four. Before revealing the details, let's first clarify the overall response strategy that Hank and you used at the town meeting.

6.

a counterintuitive strategy for saving your good idea

h ANK, WITH YOUR HELP, used a method, and a specific set of responses all based on that methodology, for gaining strong buy-in for a good idea. And it worked, as it does in real life.

The same single method worked on shots based on all of the attack strategies. You did not even have to use (and learn and master) four methods: one for confusion, another for death by delay, yet another for anxiety, and a last one for ridicule. Because there is only one response methodology, Hank, though skillful, did not have to be su-perhuman. This is also a reason that you were able to learn and start to be helpful as quickly as you did.

The method has only a handful of interrelated ele-ments, none of which is complicated. Those elements work together to achieve buy-in by

—capturing peoples' attention;

—then with people paying attention, winning over
their minds;

—and with people paying attention, also winning over
their hearts.

The most basic and counterintuitive of the elements is
the first.

**Don't scheme to keep potential opponents, even
the sneakiest attackers, out of the discussion. Let
them in. Let them shoot at you. Even encourage
them to shoot at you!**

It would seem logical, when you don't want an idea to
be shot down, that you should try to keep the shooters
away from the proposal while you are developing sufficient support to get it accepted and then used. Somehow, keep Pompus and Divertus from coming to the
meeting. Don't include Heidi on the e-mail correspon-
dence. Have hallway conversations behind Lookus's
back. With no idea killers around, there are no bullets, or
very few, and sensible proposals are much more easily
embraced and implemented.

People sometimes use this approach with a good
degree of success. But we have observed an alternative
that can be much more powerful. The approach turns the
very problem of good ideas drawing attacks to your
advantage. It does this by solving the single biggest

challenge people face when they need to gain buy-in for a good idea: simply getting people's attention.

Without people's attention, you really won't have a chance to explain a hazard or an opportunity, along with your good, practical solution. Distracted people will ignore you. They won't listen carefully or long enough. They won't listen with an open mind. You won't have the chance to gain the emotional commitment that is at the core of true buy-in. And these problems caused by a lack of attention are commonplace, for a number of perfectly understandable reasons.

Think about it. Almost all of us are overwhelmed with literally thousands of communications vying for our attention. Messages from friends, bosses, family, and colleagues via e-mail and cell phone, TV, the Internet, newspapers, and magazines—they all combine to create an impossible information overload. As a result, most messages never make it with clarity into our minds or never make it successfully without distortion.

In a typical day, we can be bombarded with six requests and four complaints from our family before 7:30 a.m., fourteen things to remember from the radio program we listen to going to our jobs, and five messages on our cell phone. As soon as we sit down at work (or pick up our BlackBerry), there may be twenty e-mails filled with information, instructions, questions, and requests. And it isn't even 9:00 a.m. yet!

People who study this problem tell us that in a week, we can be hit with 10,000 suggestions, ideas, proposals, or demands. The ideas come in written, verbal, and visual form. Ten thousand times fifty-two weeks a year adds up to a mind-boggling 520,000 proposals, plans, or ideas a year, some superb, others good, many bad, a significant number ridiculous, and some dangerous. Let's say you personally have 20 really good or important ideas this year. For other relevant people, those 20 are a drop of water in a tidal wave of 519,980 other plans, ideas, and proposals. So what are the odds that your good thoughts and suggestions will even be noticed, much less thoughtfully examined and then adequately supported? Even if you are standing in front of someone, having a personal conversation, with the information overload clogging his or her brain, how much will this person listen carefully and evaluate thoughtfully any idea that he or she has not already accepted and supported?

The method used by you and Hank dealt with this huge attention problem in the following way. First, you didn't try to keep anyone away from the meeting, even Pompus Meani. Yes, you had little time, but you're enterprising. You or Hank could have come up with some creative scheme to delay Pompus at work or divert him to some other important matter. Using this same method in other settings, we have seen people scheduling teleconferences when a disruptive George is unavailable. We have seen them hint to Jessica that it would be best if she were to keep her mouth shut this time. But you didn't do any of this.

Second, you also didn't try to silence anyone who came to the library meeting. You did just the opposite.

You allowed everyone to express an opinion or ask a question, including those you may have suspected would unfairly shoot at the computer proposal. You did not just draw out those who asked intelligent questions that can be easily answered when an idea makes sense. You didn't try to control the proceedings by creating a scripted (and possibly very boring) interaction. You didn't make a long speech and allow little time for questions and answers. You didn't ignore the raised hands of people you guessed might attack your idea. In different settings, we have observed some people use the same strategy by not only writing a memo but actively soliciting reactions to it. Instead of only e-mail, they use a chat room. Instead of a one-sided support document, they plainly include and address the alternate views that are out there, including unfair, biased, and illogical views.

At the library meeting, your approach (inevitably) led to attacks from anxious, confused, disruptive, angry, self-centered, insecure, power-hungry, or just plain skeptical people. As a result, some drama was added to what could have been a boring meeting. A few sparks flew around the room. A virtue of drama and sparks is that *they attract attention.*

When people are paying attention, their minds become engaged. That's a crucial requirement for understanding an idea and for overcoming incorrect impressions. You can then use that attention to your advantage in gaining the intellectual and emotional commitment that is at the heart of real support.

Don't try to overcome attacks with tons of data; logic and yet more logic; or lists of reasons why unfair, uninformed, or sneaky attacks are wrong, wrong, wrong. Instead, do what might seem to be the opposite.

It seems obvious: if you have done your homework and someone is trying to shoot down your good idea, you should simply use all your knowledge and data to defuse the bombs that come with confusion, delay, fear, or ridicule strategies. So you go over the proposal again. You explain why it is a good proposal. You point out all the flaws in the attack. You offer all the evidence you can think of to support your assertions. And to make sure the sneaky ploy or seemingly sensible but flawed concern is put aside forever, you offer still more evidence and more logic, essentially, shooting the attack sixteen times, assuring that it is dead.

Most of us have been trained to think this way. Indeed, almost all education teaches us to think in this manner.

An approach of overwhelming others with data and logic certainly sounds reasonable and certainly can be successful some of the time. But a potential danger is that it can inadvertently make it hard to develop—indeed can even kill—the very quality that must be present in order to build strong buy-in for an idea: crucial attention.

As you go through your list of points, your logic, your framing of the problem, your assessment of the basic alternatives and their inferiority, minds will wander. People start to think, What was I supposed to pick up at the drugstore? Am I really ready for my own presentation in the next meeting? The man sitting in front of me is developing a bald spot. Am I? I can't believe Shirley dresses that way. How long is this meeting going to last, anyway? The list of items roaming through people's heads grows while attention shrinks—and the opportunity to win people's minds slides, too.

We've all seen this many times. Eyes glaze over or look away. People surreptitiously start e-mailing or texting. Two people over to the left start whispering to each other. Someone starts doodling. Another person writes notes, but they have nothing to do with the twelve reasons why your point of view is valid.

You and Hank avoided this trap by using *almost the opposite strategy*. Your responses—all of them—were short, allowing no time for minds to wander. (If you doubt this, flip the pages back and look at the dialog. Count the number of Hank's lines. Your lines.) Your responses were also always clear—no jargon or complex arguments. And whenever possible, you used common sense rather than data or lists to make your point.

Because your responses were both brief and easy to understand, they helped clear the room of fog created by any confusion attacks from the audience. Without the fog, and with attention retained, you had a real chance, over the course of the meeting, to educate the audience in what the computer idea was and why it was a good idea—slowly but steadily winning over minds and build-ing buy-in. And that's exactly what happened.

Great leaders throughout history have understood this point about clarity, simplicity, and common sense aston-ishingly well. Whether it's Mahatma Gandhi or Sam Wal-ton, these people have taken good ideas and made them understandable for nearly everyone. These leaders are remarkably clear in what they tell us. They are beacons of common sense. With clarity, simplicity, and steadfast common sense in the face of a complex, changing world, they hold attention, win over minds, create strong sup-port, and ultimately mobilize action to achieve important ends, no matter the difficulties.

An interesting question: if simple and commonsense answers such as the ones you and Hank used can be so powerful in cases where buy-in is needed, why don't we all use them more often? Here is a guess.

Our well-educated population is too often taught to be suspicious of a simple response to any issue and to ex-pect jargon-filled rhetoric, even though it is unclear. We have been told that the world is complex (which is true) and therefore that adequate solutions should be equally complex (which is not necessarily true). Multifaceted so-lutions, in turn, would seem logically to require a sophisti-cated communication, but this often merely means obscure words, professional jargon, and long, meander-ing sentences and paragraphs.

And in a world of we-hate-them lawyers, Dilbert-ian corporations, and bizarre government bureaucracies, we are often taught by our experiences that common sense may be a casualty of the modern age. We may feel that this is unfortunate, perhaps tragic, but we have been taught that it is a reality. You cannot fight it. But in fact, you can. In a sense, we may just need to be de-programmed.

Don't try to crush attackers with ridicule, counterattacks, or condescension, even when it seems as though people deserve it, even when a part of you really wants to do just that, and you have the skills to do so.

Hank relied on this rule in every single interaction. You struggled at first because you were nervous, then mad. But you bit your tongue, then started acting like Hank. How important was that to the outcome of the meeting? It was immensely important. How important is this to what we have observed in our studies? Critical.

You need to win hearts and minds to gain true buy-in. Simple, clear, and commonsense responses can do much to win the minds. Respect can do much to win hearts.

It is difficult to overstate the negative effects caused by an attitude of disrespect. It can draw attention, but not the kind you want. You lose buy-in, rather than gaining it.

Regular, everyday people attack proposals all the time, for all sorts of conscious and unconscious reasons. There-fore, treating anyone with even a modicum of disrespect risks a backlash from the person or, more importantly, from the audience. The audience might see you as unfair or unjust. This raises the same questions about values and character that give power to character assassination and ridicule strategies.

Reacting to an obvious bully by being a bigger bully, dodging bullets and then shooting bigger bullets back, dealing with angry attacks by serving even angrier responses—any actions on your part that aggressively belittle even genuinely unkind attackers—can make an audience sympathetic to those attackers. Or your bullets can inadvertently spray around the room, as when you imply with frustration that change is needed because only Neanderthals refuse to adapt to new circumstances (and therefore that some in the audience, who don't quickly embrace change, must be Neanderthals!). Or where you are tricked into saying that traditional values are irrelevant today (and thus that some people in the audience are clinging with ridiculous tenacity to the wrong values!). Shooting back at attackers may be emotionally satisfying for a few moments. But that satisfaction tends to be fleeting.

Under most conditions that we have observed, enthusiastic support from large numbers of people is rarely if ever the product of a fight, unless those who attack an idea really are behaving outrageously. When we are furious with someone, he or she can look like a thug. But the reality is that very few people are. The head of marketing and ornery Uncle George may be maddening at times, but they are not bad people. In a difficult week, it may feel as if we are dealing constantly with idiots who deserve no respect. But that is just a feeling, not a reality.

In an attempt to gain buy-in, treating others in just the opposite way—with clear respect—allows you to take the high ground. Sympathy does not go to the attackers. Often, those trying to shoot down an idea will seem, in contrast, like mudslingers, narcissists, or just plain bullies. No one likes, or trusts, any of those sorts of people. Their character is questioned, not yours.

By treating others with respect, you draw an audience emotionally to your side, where they are more likely to listen carefully and sympathetically. In a world of information overload, where it is difficult to draw people's attention, having people genuinely listen to your message is a significant victory. Having them listen with a sympathetic attitude is a *huge victory.*

Sympathy is a feeling. Like all feelings, it is linked to what we so often call "the heart." When respect draws a sympathetic response, you are, so to speak, winning over the heart.

We aren't talking about pandering or behavior that looks weak and might logically raise the question, Are you behaving in a meek way because you know your idea is not that strong? One normally needs to be respectfully firm with a Pompus. Depending upon the other person, more or less warmth, or more or less logic, might be appropriate. But in virtually all cases, disrespect is a great risk.

Behaving with respect is always possible, despite a hardwired tendency in all of us toward fighting, running away, or becoming defensive when attacked. The first two tendencies probably made a great deal of sense when we were equipped with a sturdy wooden spear and saw a large beast while out hunting. In the twenty-first century, we don't throw spears or flee, but we do easily become defensive (sort of holding our ground but waving at, or speaking defiantly to, the other person). The more we remember that these dysfunctional behaviors pop out easily, the easier it is to monitor our feelings and keep them in check.

More so, feeling calmly self-confident is key to keeping all these unhelpful actions at bay. And self-confidence is greatly helped by the final element of an effective response strategy, preparation, which we will get to in just a minute.

Don't focus on the attacker and his or her unfair, illogical, or mean argument (though it will be extremely tempting to do so).

It is natural, when hit with confusion, fear mongering, character assassination, or delay strategies, to focus one's attention on the attacker or attackers. From our observations, we conclude that this is a big mistake. At the risk of stating the obvious, you are seeking the support and buy-in of a large fraction of the people involved, whether that means five people or fifty thousand people, whether it is around the sort of small decisions we make each day or some huge change effort that may take five years in an organization. In both cases, the key to success lies not in winning the hearts and minds of all those who, for whatever reasons, are inclined to try to shoot down a good idea. Rather, it's the thoughts and feelings of *the majority* that determine whether you win or lose the day. This simple insight leads to a fourth part of an effective response strategy: watch the crowd very carefully.

Don't be pulled into a debate where you focus on a small number of disruptive debaters instead of the large number of judges. Don't become obsessed with the one obnoxious (but clever) heckler. Don't waste your time trying to convert a minority that is so emotionally committed to an ideology that they will never support your idea unless it is changed to fit that ideology. If you know that a small group will lose something if your idea is accepted and they are tough people who never want to lose, don't try to change their personalities or values. You can't. When you are responding to an attack, the reactions of the *majority* are the real issue, not the look of pleasure or dislike on the face of the attackers. Pay insufficient attention to the majority, and you may never realize that they are confused, afraid, or being drawn into a delay—or at least you may not realize it quickly enough.

Hank (and eventually you, too) watched the audience throughout the evening. You looked left, then right, at the front rows and the back. You watched for signs that you were losing people's attention. You looked for nodding heads, for smiles or frowns, for growing energy or the lack thereof.

Of course, it may be possible to pay no attention to the audience, focus on the attackers, and still achieve a

51 percent buy-in. But accepting 51 percent can be just as much of a mistake as hoping, unrealistically, for 100 percent. With 51, you may win the vote, but you are not in the slightest way guaranteed that a good idea will be implemented successfully. With weak buy-in, people may abandon a plan when they hit the first obstacle or when they hear another alternative that seems to better serve their interests (even if it really doesn't). Buy-in for just simple plans, as at our library, may require an 80 percent yes vote, with 25 percent of the people so enthusiastic that they will volunteer to take additional action to break through barriers and bring the plan to fruition.

Don't try to wing it, even if you know all the facts thoroughly, even if the idea seems bulletproof, and even if you expect a friendly audience.

In the small-stakes interactions that happen daily, you can sometimes learn to use the ideas in this book and think on your feet pretty well with only a few minutes of preparation. Remember the four attack strategies. There are only four: confusion, delay, ridicule, fear mongering. Consider your idea and audience. Which strategies might someone use, and how? Take a deep breath and remind yourself that it's okay to let them attack. It can be useful. Keep your responses simple and filled with common sense. Respect, respect, respect. Watch the audience carefully.

But when the stakes are significant, putting in time to do your homework in a smart way is more than worth the effort. Smart means not just doing a lot of work, but also doing it efficiently and wisely, which we have seen *is* possible when you use the ideas in this book.

If the stakes are high, this book, and especially the twenty-four "cheat sheets" included later, can be used as a sort of reference manual to focus your attention in a highly productive way. That's what you and Hank did in the story. In general, you look at the common attacks. You consider which ones are likely to be used in your situation. That could be four. It could be twelve. You then look at the effective generic responses. You think how they can best be tailored to your situation. For example, if it seems clear that someone could argue, with honest skepticism or a self-centered hidden agenda, that he or she had tried the idea before and it had failed, clarify what is different today or how the ideas in fact are different. Then, depending on how simple or complex the issues, you simply remember a few powerful insights, or more likely (as did Hank), you make notes.

When you have done this sort of preparation, you will not only face attackers with highly useful material at your fingertips. You will also have more self-confidence and, with that, more capacity to think on your feet (instead of being flustered and having great difficulty thinking in the moment).

Preparation can significantly build confidence and reduce your anxiety. It really can help keep under control any dysfunctional tendency to start a useless fight or a credibility-killing retreat. It can create a calmer and more self-confident feeling, which is priceless when you're faced with intended or innocent attacks. And it can reduce the time you invest in all aspects of preparation because an increasingly calm disposition makes work much more efficient.

Perhaps most of all, the preparation that builds confidence and reduces anxiety can stop that natural tendency to become defensive when hit with "What's your hidden agenda [you creep]?"; "This sounds like [something we all dislike]"; and "It's too simplistic [and you're a moron]." Many of the generic, difficult attacks are successful because we become defensive and then attack back. And once a real shooting war starts, whatever you care about becomes at risk.

This is easier than it may sound because none of these actions need be taken with absolute perfection. In a world in which most preparation for buy-in deserves a C grade, B+ preparation can lead to actions that look inspired and are most effective.

* * *

The method, in a simple summary, is this:

1. Gain people's attention by allowing the attackers in and letting them attack.

2. Then win the minds of the relevant, attentive audience with simple, clear, and commonsense responses.

3. Win their hearts by, most of all, showing respect.

4. Constantly monitor the people whose hearts and minds you need: the broad audience, not the few attackers.

5. Prepare for these steps in advance, with the ideas in this book.

One important caveat. This method, though powerful, is not guaranteed to work well in cases with a particularly aggressive, nasty opposition. But those situations with those sorts of people are, for most of us, very rare. This observation will seem hard to believe if you live in a world filled with politically malicious, highly cynical naysayers. But, in reality, for the vast majority of us, in the vast majority of circumstances, the people who will challenge and attack your idea are far from evil thugs. An evil opposition may make good drama in movies or TV, but your cousin or boss is not a mobster.

7.

twenty-four attacks and twenty-four responses

ERE WE NOW list and discuss the twenty-four attacks that we have found used quite commonly. As you will see, they all draw on one or more strategies based on confusion, fear mongering, death by delay, or ridicule and character assassination. There are many more slight variations on these twenty-four, but these two dozen seem to be the most basic and confounding.

Here, we also list an effective response to each of the twenty-four. As you can see, each is based on a strategy of being respectful and keeping your comments short, clear, and filled with common sense. Each can work even if the person is not attacking but honestly asking what seems to him or her like a good question. Each will *not* silence valid criticism, but will help stop verbal bullets from killing good ideas.

If you are in a hurry, you can scan through the list. *There is no need to study in detail any of this material now* (unless you need it immediately or would prefer to get into very useful details). But be sure to save this as a reference manual. A shorthand version is also available online at www.kotterinternational.com/buyin or just search for Kotter and Buy-In to find the list of these twenty-four tactics.

Here we put the twenty-four into three sections based on the implicit attitude of the attacker:

1. "We don't need your idea, because the 'problem' it 'solves' doesn't exist."

2. "Okay, a problem exists, but your solution isn't a good one."

3. "Okay, a problem exists and your solution is a good one, but it will never work *here!*"

We'll also insert a few short real-life stories to illustrate the method in different contexts.

We don't need your idea, because the "problem" it "solves" doesn't exist.

1.

"We've been successful, so why change?!"

ATTACK:
We've never done this in the past, and things
have always worked out okay.

RESPONSE:
True. But surely we have all seen that those who
fail to adapt eventually become extinct.

The question of "We've done well, so why change?" is perhaps the most fundamental of all when a new idea is offered, especially in a setting with no crisis. Warning 1: this question (like all the twenty-four) can shoot down a genuinely fabulous idea. Warning 2: anyone who clearly sees the need for change can hear attack number 1 as moronic and treat the person asking the question accordingly—which is a big mistake.

There are many ways to try to honestly deal with this question, the vast majority of which are not helpful. Most responses drag you into a level of detail that can create endless debate. What is success? How do you measure it? How has the world changed? What data do you have to prove this change has occurred? Even with change, why won't the "proven ways" still work? To answer all the questions, you could respond with a fifty-two-page "business case," and people do, and it sometimes works. But what can seem like a solid, fifteen-point response can also easily put some people on the defensive. Defensive people often hurl all sorts of additional attacks.

The best response seems to be something simple, accurate, and basic: essentially, "life evolves, and to continue to succeed, we must adapt." Everyone knows this fact (the Roman Empire and General Motors being cases in point) and can be gently reminded, if necessary, with well-known examples or more specific ones known by the audience.

2.

"Money (or some other problem a proposal does not address) is the only real issue."

ATTACK:

Money is the issue, not . . . (computers,
product safety, choice of choir songs, etc).

RESPONSE:

Extra money is rarely what builds truly great
ventures or organizations.

In one form or another, money (often "the budget") is always raised when you talk of something expansive and new. One form is "Money is the real issue; your concern is not."

A money attack is tricky for many reasons. First, money *is* almost always a significant issue because resources are always limited. Second, money easily becomes an emotional issue. Third, like attack 1, this can drag you into an endless, unhelpful discussion about numbers, numbers, and more numbers. And the discussion easily wanders away from your idea and into a black hole. "Why are our revenues down? I think that's because . . . " "Marketing got a budget increase of ten percent, we got six percent. This makes no sense, and let me explain why." There is no way that you can be prepared for all possible ensuing arguments and statistics thrown your way—it's inevitable you will seem unprepared, which chips away at your credibility. And before you know it, you've lost control of the discussion, your proposal and its merits are lost in the fog, and people become irritable.

You need to dispatch money-is-the-real-issue attacks quickly and bring the conversation back to your idea or plan. One way is with a powerful, and again simple, truth: yes, more funding would be nice, but great organizations, products, or activities rarely come from a money-is-the-real-problem attitude. Examples are everywhere: Steve Jobs working in a garage; Thomas Edison without fifty PhD scientists; George Washington with a hugely underfunded army.

3.

"You exaggerate the problem."

ATTACK:

You are exaggerating. This is a small issue for us
if it is an issue at all.

RESPONSE:

To the good people who suffer because of this
problem, it certainly doesn't look small.

One basic way to attack the need to deal with any issue is to argue that it is trivial. "We are all busy. We have better ways to use our time than . . ." A smart person can debate you to death this way by raising issue after issue after issue that arguably needs just as much, if not more, attention.

Another simple, accurate, powerful truth can draw the discussion back to the merits of your idea. It draws upon our capacity to empathize or at least sympathize with others.

Virtually all new ideas are, in one form or another, trying to help people. Saying something is trivial, or implying that a problem is trivial, basically says that those people and their needs, hopes, or pains are trivial. Reframed that way, this attack usually loses its power and can raise questions about the attacker's motives rather than yours.

And it never hurts to have available the presence or voice of someone whose problems are being implicitly trivialized. Almost anyone can empathize with a cause if confronted with a real live person who has suffered and will benefit from the change. Remember Melinda from chapter 2—the teenager whose only access to computers would be the Centerville Library.

the coffee machine

A small Denver sales office of a well-known company had a coffee room with a contraption that made far-from-gourmet coffee. Everyone who took a cup put fifty cents in a jar, and it all worked out except for the undeniable fact that the coffee wasn't very good. A few employees had an idea. Let's put in a high-quality cup-at-a-time, grind-and-brew vending machine for truly outstanding coffee at only a dollar a cup. The vending company would put the machine in and maintain it at no extra cost. What's not to like?

They sent out an e-mail to everyone in the office, and up popped attack number 3, "You are exaggerating. This is a small issue for us if it is an issue at all."

You see, in their enthusiasm, the group making the proposal had not paused to consider that someone might come out in defense of the current rather sad brew. Not wise. Rare is the proposal that does not elicit opposition. In this case, if they had thought about it, they would have realized that *someone* must be responsible for the current coffee—in this case, it was Joan, the well-liked receptionist—and Joan immediately sent out a universal e-mail message that almost killed the plan.

The original proposal had the subject line "Better coffee," and Joan's response had the subject line "Better coffee is down the street." Joan's message read "I buy our coffee from a good supplier, and I regularly clean our coffee maker, which has made pretty good coffee for as long as I can remember. This is the first 'complaint' I have ever received. If you want 'perfect' coffee, just stop at the nearby Starbucks on your way in. Personally, I prefer ours. And besides, most of us are swamped with work, so why are we writing e-mails about coffee? Let's move on."

Ouch! This put the group in an awkward position. They had unintentionally insulted a terrific employee, and they now looked like a small band of self-centered elitist complainers. And Joan was right, the office was under pressure with a large workload and limited resources.

The suggested form of response to attack 3 is "To the good people who suffer because of this problem, it certainly doesn't look small." And remember, the method described in this book calls for *always showing respect* when delivering this response (and all the others, too).

If this had been a more important matter, it would have been better to move the discussion to a personal setting, as e-mail is such a problematic medium for dealing with disagreement. But the group felt a meeting would make too big a deal of this. It was only coffee, after all. And everyone was busy. So they discussed the best e-mail response over lunch and drafted it carefully.

Their subject line read "Better coffee—let's give it a try." It was addressed to Joan and copied to all:

Joan, those are excellent points. Although it must have sounded rather unappreciative of us for all the help you have volunteered over the years to assure that we had any coffee, we didn't mean it to be that way. And you're also right that there are coffee shops nearby. But some of us are budgeting pretty seriously these days, and for those who are, expensive coffee isn't a great option. And on a cold, stormy day, being forced to go outside for a nice warm brew is pretty harsh and takes time away from, as you say, a pretty big workload. Sure, this isn't a life-and-death issue, but for our Starbucks fans—and there are quite a few, and they are good folks like the rest of us—it is not a small issue, either. So what's the harm in trying the new plan? We can keep the old machine and go back to it whenever we want. We'd really like to give this a try. And this will give you a well-deserved break (you work hard enough even without coffee duties!).

Well, it was a risky move to do this by e-mail, but it succeeded! Within a few minutes, there was quite a bit of e-mail chatter containing comments like "thanks, Joan," and "why not try it," and a positive consensus emerged. And it all worked out fine.

4.

"You're implying that we've been failing!"

ATTACK:

If this is a problem, then what you are
telling us is that we have been doing
a lousy job. That's insulting!

RESPONSE:

No, we're suggesting that you are doing
a remarkably *good* job without the needed
tools (systems, methods, laws, etc.), which,
in our proposal, you will have.

Anything that might possibly be interpreted as an attack on the capabilities of others (even though that is not even remotely the case) invites a counterattack. And new ideas can easily seem to suggest that someone isn't doing his or her job. If those others aren't liked or respected, the bullets from this sort of attack might bounce off you. But as in the library story, the people who would benefit are usually entirely capable and hardworking. They're simply suffering from a less-than-optimal situation (in this case, poor equipment).

One effective response to this attack is to reposition either-or with both-can-be-true. There is nothing inconsistent with the assumption that people *are* competent *and* your proposal is needed. More is needed than their personal competence to make the activity or organization function well. More is needed to make them function as well as they could. And the "more," or at least a part of it, is your idea or proposal.

5.

"What's the hidden agenda here?"

ATTACK:

It's clear you have a hidden agenda and
we would prefer that you take
it elsewhere.

RESPONSE:

Not fair! Just look at the track record of
the good folks behind this proposal! (And
why would you even suggest
such a thing?)

Sometimes it will be subtle and sometimes not, but often you will be accused of making up a problem in order to push an idea for your personal benefit. We've all seen enough hidden agendas in life that if we are at all skeptical about a proposal, we might wonder if a hidden agenda is involved. And that is why this attack can be damaging.

You can start your response with a friendly, relaxed "Well, no." Getting defensive yourself is an easy trap here and very unhelpful. Then work off a simple fact: any good proposal will have some supporters who have good reputations or who are well liked. In this case, they are the shields that keep the bullets from doing harm.

"Surely you are not suggesting that [highly respected] Barry is lying to us about his motives." Served lightly and with no disrespect, an honestly skeptical person will think, "Good point," and back away. And a self-serving schemer will be put in a position where it is hard to press the issue.

Okay, there is a problem, but your idea is not the solution.

6.

"What about this, and that,

and this, and that . . . ?"

ATTACK:

Your proposal leaves too many questions
unanswered. What about this and that,
and this and that, and . . .

RESPONSE:

All good ideas, if they are new,
raise dozens of questions that cannot
be answered with certainty.

A common way to shoot down any new idea is to raise dozens of questions, most of which cannot be answered well, because the idea is new and therefore has not been tried before. The attacker may even feign support—"I want this to succeed, which is why you should answer [a million questions] before commencing." If not death by delay, after twenty questions shooting at the proposal from twenty different angles, then this tactic is at least death by confusion.

The best response in this case is first to gently cut off any attempt by an attacker to hit a crowd with fifty questions. Don't allow a confusion or fear-mongering strategy to work. Then be appreciative of the concerns (respect!)—because they may seem very logical to the anxious, the risk averse, and the highly skeptical. And then point out another simple truth: all new ideas may raise many more questions than can be answered with certainty. That's the very nature of a simple new idea or a grand new vision. History will never provide data that leads to 100 percent certainty that a new idea will work. But living life with a standard of nothing-new-without-100-percent-certainty will kill off many ideas that could greatly benefit us. In challenging times, it could lead to disaster.

7.

"Your proposal goes too far/doesn't go far enough."

ATTACK:
Your proposal doesn't go nearly
far enough.

RESPONSE:
Maybe, but our idea will get us started
moving in the right direction and will
do so without further delay.

"Doesn't go far enough" or "Goes too far" are common attacks that apply to almost any issue. They work when they have some minimal face-validity and when the proposal should not or cannot be adjusted easily to "go further" or "go less far."

An effective response in either case will present several ideas: (1) Good, we agree there is a problem. (2) I'm glad to see that we agree that the direction proposed is in fact the right direction. (3) So let's get started, at least. (4) If the proposal goes too far, we will see that at some point and slow down and stop. We (including you, Mr. Attacker) are smart enough to do this. (5) If it doesn't go far enough—doesn't fund the project properly, for example—this, too, will be eventually clear. We then would use whatever successes we would have had to date—and if it's a good idea, there will always be some successes—in order to mobilize people into keeping the effort going.

8.

"You have a chicken-and-egg problem."

ATTACK:
You can't do A without first doing B,
yet you can't do B without first doing A.
So the plan won't work.

RESPONSE:
Well, actually, you can do a little bit of A,
which allows a little bit of B, which allows more A,
which allows more of B, and so on.

Problems can seem unsolvable when framed as the old "without a chicken there can be no egg, yet without an egg there can be no chicken." So you're stuck. No sensible action is possible.

It helps greatly to anticipate this problem in advance and to start working on the solution before an attack can come at you. Almost always, the answer is to push along two or more activities at the same time. So you don't even try to embark upon and finish some single activity. You create a little of A, which is possible without a completed B. Then you do a little B, which is certainly possible with only support from a little, uncompleted A. And so on, with small steps over time. What looks like an unrealistic idea really is realistic.

Example: You can't invest in a college course until it is clear that enough students will take it. Yet you can't attract the students until the course is available. So you seem to be stuck. But no, there is a way out. You start small and expand. A small investment produces a small seminar, which only needs fifteen students, who will surely sign up if the idea is a good one. When the seminar is seen to be interesting, because it was a good idea, its small success will attract more students the next time. The dean then sees the justification to allocate resources to turn the seminar into a small course. The success of the small course . . . And so on.

9.

"Sounds like [something most people dislike] to me!"

ATTACK:
Your plan reminds me of a bad thing
(insert totalitarianism, organized crime,
insanity, disease, dry rot . . .).

RESPONSE:
Look, you know it isn't like that.
A realistic comparison
might be . . .

You would think that comparing an excellent plan to something unconnected and undesirable would immediately backfire, but instead, such images often stick in our minds and therefore do harm. Worse, you can do even more harm by overreacting. So quickly dismiss the comparison for what it is. Then replace a harmful image with one that is undeniably compelling, simple, and attractive—so it helps, again, to have one prepared in advance.

Example: "You're trying to shove this down our throats. What is this, Russia under Stalin?!"

"Let's be sensible. Stalin killed twenty to forty million people. So I don't think that's exactly a fair comparison.

We are being assertive. I admit that. But it's because we believe so much in this plan. A better comparison might be a person who has a good idea. His fellow employees must buy into it, or it won't be used. But they all have a hundred things on their minds and are running to the next meeting. So he does have to stand up on a soapbox and speak louder than normal. That's all.

"Is there another question or concern?" And you move on.

10.

"You're abandoning our core values."

ATTACK:

You are abandoning our
traditional values.

RESPONSE:

This plan is essential to *uphold*
our traditional values.

This can be a challenging attack. What are you going to say, that our traditional values no longer matter or that this isn't about values? There is usually no win there.

An effective response is based on a simple insight. Much more often than not, a really good idea upholds key values in the face of change.

"So, our proposal does change your [employment practices, computer systems, buildings, etc.], but this will help you maintain a key value [freedom, family, or equal opportunity].

"Yes, we propose to do advertising for the first time ever (didn't our founders hate advertising?). We think this is a good idea because it's needed to help us grow, which is essential to offering more jobs and more promotion opportunities, which has been absolutely at the core of what our founders deeply cared about. So our proposal, which might look like an abandonment of traditional values, actually is very important to uphold those values."

the acquisition

A group of retail electronic stores had for decades been in competition with another group of stores in the metropolitan area of an East Coast U.S. city. For a number of historical reasons, the employees of group 1 saw their only major competitor in the area as not just the competition, but the enemy. Then one day, unexpectedly, that other group made an offer to purchase group 1.

The man who ran group 1 studied the offer very carefully and decided for many reasons that it was mostly a good idea for people who had invested in the business, for the employees, and for the community. He knew he would need to explain his reasoning to his employees and to do it well enough that he didn't have a mutiny on his hands. For very practical reasons, he didn't want any good people quitting or morale collapsing. For personal reasons, he didn't want to lose friendships with people he had known for many years.

He was well aware that he had a few routine critics who would ask many questions. He prepared for that. He also knew that some people would undoubtedly attack the idea because they were anxious or angry, or perhaps because they cared more about their careers than what was good for the company. And he was right.

His communication strategy was to send a thoughtfully written document to all employees and follow this immediately with a series of meetings with groups of thirty or fifty of his people. The sessions were one hour long, scheduled back to back, day and night, and were run by him. In his very first meeting, he was immediately hit with attack number 10: "You are abandoning our traditional values." Someone told a story of how the other group of stores was supposedly once outrageously unfair to a customer, something "we would never do." With a voice that communicated more and more indignation every minute, the attacker said the proposal would "sell us down the drain. What we have stood for will disappear. What our founder cared so much about will be lost. How could you even think of doing this?!" People at the meeting who had been cautiously nodding their heads in response to the proposal immediately stopped. The attack was working.

The most "logical" (and ineffective) response would have been to blow this concern away: "Chances are overwhelming that's an isolated incident from an earlier era. You could probably find one similar, worrisome story about us out there, too." But the attacker had raised fears in the audience, the sort of feelings that are not necessarily soothed by a simple, logical response. And then the boss could be in trouble.

The suggested response to attack 10 is of the form "This plan is essential to uphold our traditional values."

Knowing this response, and having thought about it in his preparation for these meetings, the boss in this case said, "You are correct on one part. I think all of us care deeply about serving our customers well. But whether we like it or not, huge national chains are moving into areas like ours and they don't necessarily have those same feelings. But they are very good at competition. Their large size gives them lower costs in buying and lower prices for consumers. As we have seen in the national media, some companies like ours have been put out of business. And then we would really abandon our values.

"The combined forces of our firm and our longtime competitor can help us survive and may even stop one of the big chains from coming here in the first place. So the acquisition would help us not to lose our traditional values. It could help us maintain them."

Of course, this was just one scene in a complex story. But it's a good example of response 10 defeating attack 10, and in a setting very different from our Centerville Library.

11.

"It's too simplistic to work."

ATTACK:

Surely you don't think a few
simple tricks will solve everything?

RESPONSE:

No, it's the combination of your good work
and some new things that, together,
can make a great advance.

At some point, a few simple components of your plan may seem to stand out and, to some, may seem to "be" your plan. Opponents can seize on this. So they say, correctly, that those few elements are too simplistic to solve the problem.

For example, they might criticize increasing the size of a police force by saying, "Guns and badges won't stop crime." The best response often emphasizes the combination of new and existing elements, including the current "talented police officers."

So, you say something like "That's undoubtedly true, but that is not what we are proposing. It's the combination of the force's systems, structures, our new prevention activities, excellent people, and additional help that will make the difference." This is true, undermines "simplistic," and puts an attacker in the position that any comeback may sound like he or she does not think the current force is "excellent," a risky proposition at best with police officers and their friends in the audience.

12.

"No one else does this!"

ATTACK:

If this is such a great idea, why
hasn't it been done already?

RESPONSE:

There really is a first time for everything, and we do
have a unique opportunity.

A very reasonable question is, If this new proposal is good, why don't we see others using it? Surely someone would be.

A good response is simple. "Any idea has to be used a first time. That's common sense. So why not us?"

If you are asking for something dangerously risky or very expensive, this response probably won't work—at least by itself. Sometimes the added line is just, How do you know? The world is a very big place, and someone could be implementing your idea right now and you wouldn't know it.

If the attacker is being aggressively nasty, you can take your response to the point that it suggests the attacker seems to be insulting your organization, community, or group. "You are saying that we/you have no capacity to innovate? To ever do anything on the leading edge? That we/you must forever meekly follow others? Frankly, that sounds sort of insulting to me."

Of course, if you *know* you will be hit with this attack, go look for some person or company who has used your idea (or something close) before.

13.

"You can't have it both ways!"

ATTACK:
Your plan says X and Y, but they are
incompatible. You can't have both!

RESPONSE:
Actually, we didn't say X or Y—although,
I grant you, it may have sounded
that way. We said A and B, which
are not incompatible.

Often, someone will distort two things you have said to build an apparent contradiction. Such an attack can be very effective because, as the attacker frames the issue, he or she *is* correct.

For example, "You said this equipment would not be expensive, but later you acknowledged it will have to be strong, which will logically cost more money. What do you want, strong or cheap? You can't have it both ways!"

In a case like this, the best response is to be understanding and to gently point out their error. Something can be "not too expensive" and "not too weak," which is what your proposal actually says, and that is entirely different than saying both "strong" and "cheap."

paving the alley

He was just out of college, in his first job, and he and his spouse lived in a quiet residential area that included an unpaved road (actually, a small lane). The road had very little traffic (just a few neighbors took it once or twice a day), and so the neighborhood children often played various games there. And they had a great time. The local government offered a very good program to pave such lanes in order to improve appearances and keep down dust. If neighbors agreed to sign up, they just paid a little more tax for a few years (and we mean very little). This man called a meeting in his own home to explain why he felt this was a good idea and why the neighbors should sign up. He argued that it would improve land values, it would make the road less bumpy to drive on, and it would be great for the kids playing games, especially basketball.

And then came attack 13: "You can't have it both ways." In this case, it was from a Heidi Agenda.

Heidi could easily afford the very minor additional cost, but she was pathologically cheap and didn't want to admit it. Instead, she concocted an impressively reasoned attack. She pointed out that the man said the paved road would make it nicer for cars—hence, a veritable speedway. (But, of course, the man never said speedway.) She then observed that the man claimed it would be wonderful for children—basically a nicely paved playground. (And of course, he never said playground.) And so, she told her neighbors, this can't be a speedway and a playground at the same time! So what is the proposal?

The general answer to attack 13 is always to point out, politely, that you *didn't say* "oil" and "water," which usually don't go together. What you *did say* was "olive oil" and "vinegar," which make a fine salad dressing.

The young man stayed calm and remembered that it is always a distortion of what people say that generates such an attack. Respectfully fix the distortion, and the attack disappears. In a matter-of-fact tone, he pointed out that he did not say that he expected cars to drive on the paved road more often or faster, simply that it would be a nicer experience. (And by the way, he noted, speed bumps can solve a problem if it arose, which was highly unlikely.) And he never suggested that children should treat the road like an actual playground, but the fact was that children had been playing on that quiet lane for many decades and no one had ever come even close to getting hurt by a car. So, yes, the lane can be nicer for drivers and nicer for children at the same time.

They paved the alley. It certainly wasn't a cure for a dreaded disease, but it was an improvement to the neighborhood nevertheless. And one by one by one, these sorts of improvements add up in surprising ways.

14.

"Aha! You can't deny this!" ("This" being a worrisome thing that the proposers know nothing about and the attackers keep secret until just the right moment.)

ATTACK:

I'm sorry—you mean well, but look at this problem you've clearly missed! You can't deny the significance of this issue!

RESPONSE:

No one can deny the significance of the issue you have raised, and yes, we haven't explored it. But every potential problem we have found so far has been readily solved. So in light of what has happened again and again and again, I am today confident that this new issue can also be handled, just like all the rest.

This is the "gotcha" problem. It usually has an element of undeniable truth and is often deliberately kept secret from you so it can be used to embarrass you at the worst moment. Caught off guard, you can be left stumbling, which is what the attacker wants. But there is an effective response that will work virtually all the time.

First, go ahead and point out, honestly, that you are indeed hearing this for the first time. Trying in seconds to come up with a great solution to the new problem suggested by the new information is risky, at best. So don't try.

Then say that quite honestly, you will have to look into the issue. But, point out a simple and logical truth. For every other issue that you have studied, you have found a solution. In light of that *fact*, is it really unreasonable to say that the same will happen in this case? So thanks for alerting us to the potential problem, George, and, by the way, thank all of you here who have already alerted us to problems—which have all since been solved.

15.

"To generate this many questions and concerns, the idea has to be flawed."

ATTACK:
Look at how many different concerns
there are! This can't
be good!

RESPONSE:
Actually, if there are many questions,
that's good, because it shows we are engaged,
and an engaged group both makes better
decisions and implements them
more successfully.

This attack can be tricky to counter because too many concerns can be the sign of a real problem. But more often, this tactic is used as a means to kill a plan. The best response is, again, a simple truth.

You acknowledge the issue (showing respect) and then point out that raising many issues is actually *good*, for three reasons. First, it demonstrates that the problem or opportunity being addressed is important, or people would not put their energy into such a discussion. Everyone is busy, so we shouldn't be working on unimportant issues.

Second, much debate can be a useful test to see if what you are convinced is a good idea really is a good idea. With few concerns from those who need to buy into an idea, the idea is not really tested. You don't want untested proposals.

Third, good questions and concerns can help you to make useful adjustments to a plan that is fundamentally sound.

16.

"We tried it before—didn't work."

ATTACK:
We tried that before, and
it didn't work.

RESPONSE:
That was then. Conditions inevitably
change (and what we propose
probably isn't exactly what
was tried before).

Your plan may be new, but often someone can claim that it is not—that a plan with essentially the same characteristics was tried some time ago and failed, thus proving that your plan is doomed. "We did that back in oh-five, and look at what it got us. Nothing. And it cost . . . "

It doesn't hurt, as a part of your preparation, to learn about earlier similar efforts. Then, when hit with the attack, you acknowledge the similarities between what the situation was before and how that plan has elements of your current plan. But, you point out, if it is a good idea now, either the plan is different or the situation has changed or, more likely, both.

You could go into great detail to explain your point (or be drawn into greater detail), but that can be another trap. The attacker can keep raising issue after issue after issue, and you may not remember or know the details associated with all those issues. So point to what cannot be argued: times change and the situation today is inevitably different.

It really is that simple . . . so keep it simple.

microcharity

She was (and is still) on the board of a charitable foundation that gives grants aimed at helping inner-city residents. Because it is a relatively small foundation, the board itself had been selecting award recipients from the applications. She had become convinced that the board members were too far removed from the inner city to really understand what the most worthy small projects were. So she proposed to her fellow board members, first in a written document, then in a teleconference, that they grant a substantial portion of the money available each year to one or more existing inner-city organizations, asking them in turn to grant funds to small, local worthy causes. That way, many small decisions could be made by people who had a clear view of their potential value.

She was hit with attack 16: "We tried that before, and it didn't work." A Pompus Meani had already been working her over, and so a Bendi Windi (a male version, this time) felt compelled to chime in with his own attack. He reminded everyone that a few years before, one of the applications the agency supported was a person who intended to "subgrant" funds to community gardens. The recipient hired a consultant to study such gardens (his cousin, as it turned out), and essentially all the money went to the consultant and none to the gardens.

What to do? The woman who was attacked knew the general response to a type 16 bombshell: "That was then. Conditions inevitably change, and what we're proposing is different from what was tried before in the following ways . . ." So she respectfully pointed out that while superficially, the two situations sounded similar, they really were not. Her plan, she told them, would be to evaluate the competence of the grantee specifically with regard to the task of subgranting efficiently and effectively to worthy local recipients. That, she pointed out, was not done before. Moreover, the idea of moving decisions closer to where they matter was a much-better-understood idea than a few years back and now had been proven successful in many areas of society. "So why not give it a try?" Which they did.

Okay, there is a problem, and this is a good proposal to deal with the issue, but you'll never make it work *here*.

17.

"It's too difficult to understand."

ATTACK:

Too many of our people will never
understand the idea and, inevitably,
will not help us make it happen.

RESPONSE:

Not a problem. We will make the
required effort to convince them.
It's worth the effort to do so.

The tricky thing about this attack is that the attacker can pose as your ally. She loves your plan and wants it to happen, but sadly, the "others" will misunderstand, and that's that.

The truth is that almost anyone can understand an idea if time is spent explaining it clearly and simply. Yes, an incompetent communication effort can bog down the effort and absorb an unjustifiable amount of resources. But being clear and simple is at the heart of "competent," and clarity also tends to be remarkably efficient and is always possible. So, you might say, "Since you agree that the plan is good, then of course it's worth the effort to communicate it.

"We just need to be clear in what we say.

"And let's not allow some failed experiences in the past to make us cynical about explaining a proposal to 'them.' Our people are often smarter than you might think."

A REAL-LIFE EXAMPLE

tips and territory

In a small Southern town there is an old-time diner that has two servers on duty for most of the year, but during the busier summer months, the owner adds one more, usually a university student in need of summer employment.

Of the two regulars, Madge had been there the longest (possibly forever). And while the other, Wendy, was newer and younger, she was equally well liked. It was a good place, and the new student, Tom, was grateful for the employment and was enjoying the work.

There was just one problem. Tom had been told that he could expect tips to approximately double the minimum-wage payment he received for this work, and he needed that money. But it wasn't quite working out that way. So he started thinking things over. The three servers had each been assigned a "territory" in the restaurant, with each territory having the same number of tables. People could sit wherever they wanted. When the restaurant was full, this gave an equal number of customers, and hence tips, to each server. But Madge's section, which was nearest to the door, was where people tended to sit when the place wasn't busy, which was much of the time.

Wendy was a very sweet person, and when Tom asked her one day how she felt about the arrangement, he could tell she wasn't clear how she felt and couldn't imagine doing anything about it. She just wanted to do her job well and get on with her busy life as a single mom.

One day, Tom discussed this with his family over dinner and asked if they thought he should say something about the problem. On the one hand, he was thankful for the employment and it was just for a short time. But on the other hand, Wendy would probably be working there for a long time, and the arrangement was not fair to her, either. Tom figured there was a simple solution. The servers could just take turns with the different sections, which would also add a little variety. But how does the person at the bottom of the totem pole suggest such a thing? Tom's mother asked him about the people involved, and they discussed what might happen. Tom figured it was now or never and vowed to bring this up the next day.

So in the morning, when they were all preparing to open the restaurant, Tom turned to the owner (also the cook), old Samuel Mulligan. "Mr. Mulligan," he said, "would you mind if I made a suggestion?" Which Tom then did.

As you might expect, Tom's suggestion did not appeal to Madge, as it would reduce her family income, maybe not a lot, since she had a husband who was a supervisor in a local area firm, but would reduce her tips nevertheless. And there was something about the speed of Madge's attack that made it clear she had long prepared for this moment. She lobbed a very well-aimed attack number 17 (i.e., that an idea is too difficult to understand).

She used an interesting twist: "Tom, that's a smart idea—your plan would be fairer—and that's just the kind of good idea we'd expect from a smart college student like you. But, honey, we ain't smart college folks. Wendy, bless her soul, has enough trouble keeping her orders straight already, and we have elderly customers who would find this terribly confusing. They always sit in Wendy's section, and if she suddenly isn't serving them, they will undoubtedly call her over. This would leave her real customers uncovered. She would have difficulty explaining to them why a change was needed after all these years. It would be a mess. It may sound simple to you, but the truth is, it's way too complicated to be understood by everyone here."

Well, Tom was in luck. His mother had actually predicted the "too complicated" attack, and so he was ready, in real time, to use the suggested response to attack 17, which is "Not a problem. We will make the required effort to convince them. It's worth the effort to do so."

In this case, Tom said to Madge and their boss, "Madge, honestly, I find the people in this diner and most of our customers to be smarter than many of the folks at my college, but I'll agree with you it might take a little explaining to get the new system working. But if it is a fairer system, as you say it is, then surely it's worth that little bit of extra effort for a little while. And what's the harm? We could al-ways switch back."

Well, old Sam Mulligan was a pretty sharp guy. There was a brief pause, and he said, "You're right, kid. Let's try it. Starting now."

Over the years, this made a big financial difference to Wendy and her children. And it was a very good lesson for Tom.

18.

"Good idea, but this is not the right time."

ATTACK:

Good idea, but it's the wrong time. We need to wait until
this other thing is finished (or this other thing is started,
or the situation changes in a certain special way).

RESPONSE:

The best time is almost always when you have people
excited and committed to make something happen.
And that's now.

This is often a ploy in which the opponent (once again)
pretends to like your plan, but at the *right* time. Which is
not now.

You can always find an example or two where it probably was sensible to wait until something was finished or
something else was started or the situation changed in
some way. But death by delay is so common that a good
rule of thumb, whenever you have a good idea, is to
never procrastinate.

Another attack ploy is to say, "We already have twenty-
four projects, so we can't add a twenty-fifth right now." A
good response is, "You make an excellent point. No one

can handle twenty-four projects well. We need to weed out and stop all of those that aren't as good as this plan and do so immediately." Which, when done, can be of enormous benefit, not just to your good idea but to the health of an organization.

19.

"It's just too much work to do this."

ATTACK:
This seems too hard! I'm not sure we are up for it.

RESPONSE:
Hard can be good. A genuinely good new idea, facing
time-consuming obstacles, can both raise our energy
level and motivate us to eliminate wasted time.

This attack can be powerful when people are genuinely feeling overworked and underpaid (not a rare problem these days). But, once again, there is a sensible response.

To paraphrase John F. Kennedy when he spoke of the moon mission, "we can be the ones to succeed, not because it is easy, but because it is hard." That may sound counterintuitive, but it is in fact very insightful.

While worthwhile endeavors may be hard, often they don't feel that way, because their value gives us strength. A wonderful thing about being human is that a worthwhile cause can raise us from feeling tired to feeling inspired. History shows us that inspired groups—even just a little bit inspired—can achieve more than would seem to be possible.

Here is where your description of the idea is so important. There is a big difference between "the whole idea is to upgrade the computers to MLX standard" and "this will help the librarians, who have done so much for us over the years, and will offer kids with little access to computers a crucial resource they must have to get into college or get almost any job these days."

20.

"It won't work here; we're different!"

ATTACK:

It won't work here, because we
are so different.

RESPONSE:

Yes it's true, we're different, but we
are also very much the same.

The "we're different" ploy is frequently used because it has face validity. We *are* all different. The best response is never to argue that point but to make another observation.

With a well-educated group, that observation might be, "As you know, whether it's a teenage Korean girl or an American male retiree, we all share about 99.99 percent of the same genes. In a very basic sense, people are remarkably similar all over, aren't they?" So are organizations, as anyone who has traveled the world helping customers with IT problems, for example, well knows.

As with all effective responses, a simple example, with which an audience can easily relate, is helpful. And finding that example when preparing for a meeting or writing a memo or speech is easier than you might think.

travel sanity

Franco was a sales manager working for a company that sold high-end manufacturing equipment. It was a highly specialized product, and the firm was a leader in its field. The company had major manufacturing customers all over the country. The sales were few and far between, but each sale was in the hundreds of thousands of dollars, so the cost of traveling to obtain the orders and service the sales was not a problem. And this made it possible for the sales force to be centrally located and closely in touch with the technical people, producing the "seamless full service" the company was famous for. It had a fabulously loyal customer base, which had grown to include customers in most major cities in the country. For Franco, this was a problem and an opportunity.

The problem was that the system for allocating customer accounts to the sales team was . . . well, there *was* no system, as near as he could tell. When he joined the firm, he took over for an employee who had left, and he discovered that his customer list spanned the entire country, and this was true for the other five members of the sales team as well. In some cases, different team members had customers in the same city. Franco was frustrated that so much of his time was spent traveling across the continent, instead of speaking with customers (or being with his children). While he was flying in one direction, one of his colleagues was probably flying in the other.

This was also an opportunity for Franco. If he could devise a solution, it might improve his chances of being considered for the director of sales position if it ever opened up, and it would be better for business and also for his commissions. And best of all, who would it hurt?

Well, when a bad idea has been continuing for a long time, you can bet it is in *someone's* interest. It turned out that the director of sales had considered this problem in the past, but one of the other sales managers, Larry Henderson, had always come up with a rationale to defend the status quo. The truth was that Larry didn't much like working, but loved traveling, loved the frequent-flyer miles, and loved being away from home (let's not go there), and he felt very self-important having major accounts in "every corner of the country." On top of that, Larry was absolutely sure he was next in line for the director of sales position, and he would do whatever it took to make sure that no one else would be seen as a contender.

Franco wondered what he was walking into when he worked up the courage to speak up at a sales meeting. He gave a brief, articulate summary of the problem and the recommended solution, and he mentioned the simple ways to work around the obvious issues involved in transitioning sales accounts. His presentation was clear and compelling. There were a few good-natured comments, and then, inevitably, Larry Henderson spoke. Undoubtedly, he had spent some of his long flight hours preparing for this day.

"Franco," he said in a deep, authoritative tone. He paused just long enough to make it clear he would speak further when he was certain everyone was giving him the full attention he deserved. And then, bang. He struck with attack 20, which basically says it won't work here, because we are so different. In a few carefully chosen words, it looked as if Larry were trying to humiliate Franco while derailing his idea. Here's what Larry said:

> Franco, how long have you been with us now? Six months? Oh—two years, you say! Is it really that long now? Well, I'm not sure where you were before this, but clearly you were not working for a quality supplier of electrosonic pyroconverters, and certainly not for *the premier supplier*, because there is only one premier supplier, and that, Franco, is *us*. And why are we number one? Is it because we build better product? No! Is it because our prices are lower? No! We are number one because our customers *love* us. And why do they love us? Because when they need us, we are there. We always have been. We always will be. That's our way. Well, Franco, your "sales consolidation" plan is so [he uses air quotes] "textbook" and so much like what our competitors would do. We would only

go there if someone made us lose our way. Which makes me think that if you are so fond of this idea, why don't you just take it over to one of our competitors, while we laugh all the way to the bank!

Under normal circumstances, this would be where a Franco would vow to never again speak up at meetings, which would eventually lead to Larry's getting the promotion Franco probably deserved. But not this time. Franco had actually anticipated such an attack, and he had even guessed that Larry might use such a tone.

At a moment like this, time often seems to slow down, and this gave Franco a chance to figure out a good way to phrase the suggested response to attack 20, which is basically "Yes it's true, we're different, but we are also very much the same."

All eyes were on him, as he calmly spoke, not to Larry, but to the others in the room, who he sensed often found Larry arrogantly offensive. Franco calmly said, "Well, of course, we have differentiated ourselves in important ways, but obviously, we face the same financial and time pressures as our competitors, we work in the same industry, we hire from the same labor pool, we pay the same taxes, we sell to the same customers, and we use the same sorts of accounting systems. If you think about it, the list of similarities is longer than any list of differences. And that doesn't mean that every one of the differences is necessary, perfect, or ideal. Surely, we have to be open to the possibility of improvement. We shouldn't assume improvement is impossible here because we are already so perfect or special. I propose that it is the right time to think this over, clearly, and with an open mind."

The director of sales turned to Franco and in a friendly voice said, "Good point. Send me a memo setting out what you have in mind." There were smiles around the table (except, of course, from Larry).

The memo worked, the plan worked, and the company expanded internationally. And Franco received the first of several promotions.

21.

"It puts us on a slippery slope."

ATTACK:

You're on a slippery slope leading to a cliff. This small move today will lead to disaster tomorrow.

RESPONSE:

Good groups of people—all the time—use common sense as a guard rail to keep them from sliding into disaster.

"If you make this one small move, then you will not be able to refuse the next one and the next, and so on, and this will eventually lead to disaster." It's another good attack because almost all of us can think of at least one example from our own experience where that seemed to be the case. But it doesn't have to be that way, especially if you are sensitive to the slopes and certainly if you use nothing more than common sense as a guard rail.

A good response to this attack is a counterexample with which people can obviously relate.

"We now let a ten-year-old have access to material—on TV, for example—that we would never have allowed a century ago. A reasonable crowd could debate whether that is good or bad. But there is no chance we will allow

167

this to slide into a decision that gives a ten-year-old the right to drive a car or vote in a presidential election. Although we might wonder at times, common sense does give us guard rails."

Here, you can also respectfully remind people that good organizations maintain standards through their steadfast values, judgment, and wisdom. This allows you to point out, "And we are a very good organization." Will the attacker argue with that?

22.

"We can't afford this."

ATTACK:

The plan may be fine, but we cannot do it without new sources of money.

RESPONSE:

Actually, most important changes are achieved without new sources of money.

Earlier (attack 2), we discussed the objection that the only problem is a lack of money and that your idea is focusing on a non-problem. This is different. Here, the critic acknowledges that there is both a problem and a sensible solution. But it's hopeless to implement the good idea inside our organization (or group or family), because we realistically cannot afford it unless we take funds from something that we know is needed. Just look at the budget!

The simple answer here is, sure we can: we can reprioritize; we can borrow; we can beg. The fact is, in many, many cases where a new idea has been carried out well, the money had to be found. It wasn't just sitting there. But because people had truly bought into a proposal, they just found it. People do, and all the time.

23.

"You'll never convince enough people."

ATTACK:

It will be impossible to get unanimous
agreement with this plan.

RESPONSE:

You are absolutely right. That's almost
never possible, and that's okay.

This is different from the earlier proposed problem ("others will not understand"). Here it's suggested that no matter how thoroughly the good idea is explained, there are *some* people in this organization who will simply *never* agree, and that this is a fatal problem. It is hard to argue with the first point (you won't get everyone to agree) since it's generally true. But that doesn't prove the second point (that you then have a fatal problem).

The best response, therefore, is easy. It's basically, "You're right. It's never possible to get one hundred percent consensus on anything. It's tough to get eighty percent. Yet new ideas and plans and visions become a reality all the time. So reality shows us that near total agreement is not necessary."

But never forget, a mere 51 percent raising their hands will almost never get the job done. The bigger the idea, the more people you need to buy in and do so with enthusiasm.

24.

"We're simply not equipped to do this."

ATTACK:
We don't really have the skills or credentials
to pull this off!

RESPONSE:
We have much of what we need, and
we can and will get the rest.

Margaret Mead, the world-famous anthropologist, once said, "Never doubt that a small group of thoughtful committed citizens can change the world. Indeed, it's the only thing that ever has." And she was right.

All the time, groups do not have all the skills or credentials required to implement a good idea. But they have some of them. And they somehow find a way to identify and eventually attract the rest.

By the way, some of the most thoughtful people who support your idea will often be the ones to express such self-doubts. To help them, some local examples of great success despite the initial lack of some skills could make this concept more credible.

8.

a quick reference guide for saving good ideas

S O, WHERE DOES this all lead?

From what we have observed, if you have a good idea, whether it's as small as what flavor of cake to serve at your best friend's birthday party or as large as what company to merge with, and you want to help create strong buy-in among relevant others, you can take the following four simple steps, which will save you time, boost your confidence, and greatly improve your chance of success.

step 1: take stock

First, take stock of where you are, and make sure you have not forgotten anything obvious.

It never hurts to double-check the plan: Have we really listened to feedback carefully and incorporated any good suggestions into the proposal?

Review what communications (if any) have already gone out about the plan (one-on-one talks, meetings, memos, e-mail), and evaluate how much buy-in has already been achieved. Be careful here. People tend to over-estimate how much others understand, much less embrace, a good idea. Do you really know who needs to buy in and how much they already have? What concrete evidence is available?

Ask yourself, have the tasks that communication specialists generally recommend been done?

- Have you made sure your idea is crystal clear? Can you explain it to someone in an elevator ride up to the top of the Empire State Building?

- Has anyone talked to likely supporters about the material before going into a broader discussion with the relevant community?

- If some supporters are in a more logical position to address some of the attacks, have they been asked to do so?

- Is there an overall plan about when and how to best communicate to relevant others?

- If the plan calls for a face-to-face meeting, as in the Centerville story, have you tried to role-play the meeting in advance with other supporters acting as attackers and then tried to respond, immediately, as you would have to during your actual meeting?

- Never forget that a good rule of thumb is that it's impossible to overcommunicate, using different settings and using different modes of communication.

- And so forth—a good communication professional can probably add another dozen ideas, so consider asking one.

step 2: brush up on this book

Think about the key messages of this book: the four attack strategies, the overall response strategy, and the twenty-four specific attacks and responses.

Remember that there really are just four basic attack strategies:

1. Fear mongering

2. Death by delay

3. Confusion

4. Ridicule and character assassination

And there are only a few elements in your response strategy:

—Let the attackers into the discussion, and let them go after you.

—Keep your responses clear, simple, crisp, and full of common sense.

—Show respect constantly. Don't fight or collapse or become defensive.

—Focus on the whole audience. Don't be distracted by the detractors.

—Prepare for the inevitable attacks—the bigger the stakes, the greater the preparation.

And remember, there is no reason to memorize the twenty-four specific attacks and responses. Instead, just use the listing of twenty-four attacks and responses provided in chapter 7. If the stakes are small, if there are few people that need to buy in, and if you don't have a dozen distracters, a quick flip through those pages might be sufficient. And after numerous uses of those pages, you will start to remember the most common attacks and responses. As the stakes and the numbers go up, brainstorming the possible attacks is a more worthwhile investment of time.

step 3: brainstorm possible attacks

If the stakes are big enough, always set aside time for one or more brainstorming sessions. As with any creative session, it is preferable to have a small group, not you alone. It's ideal if the group includes fairly creative people with differing outlooks. It's very helpful to go through the list of twenty-four generic forms of attack and, for each, to try to anticipate tough attacks of that general type, but in a form that is specific to your particular situation. Often when scanning the attacks, you will think of a twenty-fifth or twenty-sixth that is a slight variation on our list. A good response will probably also be a slight variation on our response.

This is actually easier than it may at first seem, because at any one time, some of the attacks won't apply, and some may be quite obvious and won't need much thought. But for those that are relevant—it could be attack 5, could be 14—creative brainstorming will be golden. You will uncover potential attacks that otherwise would have been missed, and you will discover the joy of having a respectful, effective response at your fingertips when you really need it.

As a specific example of the creative process, consider attack 16, "We tried that before, and it didn't work." If you can imagine this coming up, think about specific failures in the past that an attacker could point to in this way. The generic response is "That was then, this is now." But it will be very helpful for you to have at the top of your mind what is different now on this specific issue—preferably things that are simple and clearly true—and be prepared to express this in a way that is not disrespectful and is easily understood by the people who will be listening.

This homework needn't take long, but it is more than worth the effort because very few of us can respond well in real time to unexpected attacks. To put it another way, how often have you walked away, frustrated, from an encounter and thought, "If only I had said . . . "?

And because preparation makes you more self-confident, and your self-confidence is based on something solid, not wishful thinking, you are often able to reflect faster, in the heat of a battle, when hit with an unexpected attack.

step 4: go!

Finally, be sure to actually *use* the method we describe in this book and the responses that you devise in the brainstorming process. This point seems ridiculously obvious, yet people read and even refer to books all the time, *but don't really use them when needed*. The barrage of tasks, information, meetings, and so on that clog our days gets in the way. Don't let that happen to you.

And *never forget*: don't run away from attacks; go toward them. It will save good ideas. With significant proposals, this method may even—at least once in a while—make the world a little bit better, for us and for future generations.

ONE FINAL THOUGHT TO PUT ALL this material in perspective.

What if good ideas are crushed (1) twenty times per day in one single, big company (which, if it has ten thousand employees, is a small number of ideas) and (2) once a day for every thousand people in a country (which also sounds very small)? Do the math, and you find that's over five thousand good ideas per year shot down in a big company and over three million per year in North America. Three million good ideas a year, the best 1 percent of which—thirty thousand!—might have a very large effect on a few, or maybe most, of us.

And never underestimate the negative effect of just one major change effort's being derailed at your employer. Job losses go up, stock price goes down, quality of products or services slips, and so on. And what if it's not your employer but an organization that supplies your firm with critical software or has the mission of protecting your family against a terrorist attack?

The numbers add up. The consequences add up. And that, obviously, is not good, nor necessary.

Let's stop this needless loss.

how the method helps large-scale change

One of us (Kotter) has been studying buy-in within the very specific context of large-scale change projects for nearly two decades. Because of the increasing importance of large-scale organizational change, we feel it necessary to explicitly comment on how the work in this book fits into that context.

Research clearly shows that people, even experienced executives, are not very good at transformational change, or change of any significance. Multiple studies have shown that 70 percent of the time, when significant change is needed, people back away, go into denial, try but fail rather miserably, or stop, exhausted, after achieving half of what they want using twice the budgeted time and money.

Nevertheless, there are cases of organizations changing to exploit big opportunities, and the changes are, by most standards, sensationally successful. And, to our good fortune, in all of those cases, there is a clear pattern of what works. The pattern has eight steps.

the eight steps to successful, large-scale change

step 1: increase urgency

It all starts when large numbers of people see a big opportunity and develop a gut-level drive to get up each and every day determined to do something, however small, to help exploit that opportunity. Complacent people shed their complacency. Those who might appear urgent, because their activities are so filled with energy, but who in fact achieve little with their frenetic, anxiety-driven behavior, see the opportunity, start to think optimistically, stop running in circles, and become productive.

step 2: build the guiding coalition

With urgency high enough, a strong group of people emerges to guide the change. Within this group are some people who have credibility with others, or have connections to various parts of the organization, or leadership skills, or formal authority, and still more. Because they feel a strong sense of urgency, these people are not forced by anyone to be on a "committee" or "task force." They want to help. They volunteer to help. And they learn to work together as a team, even if they include subgroups from different parts of the organization or different locations (hence the term *coalition*).

step 3: get the vision right

The guiding coalition becomes the central force in creating a change vision and change strategies. It answers the questions, How would we look different in a few years if we were to successfully grab our biggest opportunity, and what strategies, or strategic initiatives, will get us there? And the coalition members answer those questions well, based on a solid understanding of what is changing around them, what their organization is like, and what they deeply care about.

step 4: communicate for buy-in

The coalition, still filled with a sense of urgency, finds ways to communicate the vision and strategies to everyone who needs to hear them, in order to obtain broad-based buy-in. Whatever methods needed are identified and used. Communication occurs relentlessly, typically using any channel: meetings, e-mail, papers, one-on-one conversations, posters. When enough people have truly bought in, intellectually and emotionally, the process continues.

step 5: empower action

People who buy into a vision look for ways to help the change effort without being instructed. But they almost inevitably run into some obstacles. The obstacles take many, many forms: bosses who haven't bought in; IT systems not capable of supporting the strategies; lack of the skills needed to make the vision a reality; a lack of training to develop these missing skills. The guiding coalition finds ways to eliminate these obstacles, empowering people to do what they want and what the change effort requires.

step 6: create short-term wins

Empowered people, feeling a sense of urgency and guided by the vision and strategies, focus their actions on achieving a continuing series of visible and unambiguous successes, starting as quickly as possible. With visibility to as many people as possible, and with a lack of ambiguity that makes it difficult to argue whether these are real successes on the journey to the vision, skeptics become supporters. Cynics lose their power. Momentum is gained.

step 7: keep at it

Early successes, while desirable, also create the danger of complacency. Since a few successes never take you the distance to achieve a vision of significant change, such complacency must be avoided at all costs. In successful large-scale change efforts, that problem is anticipated and effort is directed to keeping urgency up, keeping the wins coming, and never letting up until all the necessary changes have been made. Only when the organization has achieved the change vision, and only after its success is clear to all, does effort shift to the last step.

step 8: make change stick

A new order of operating is always fragile at first. Tradition is a powerful force that can pull an organization back to what it has been doing, often for years, and is comfortable with doing. In successful change efforts, work ends only after the changes have been institutionalized to make them stick. Structures, systems, and promotion processes all are set to support the new order. When a changed culture emerges, it provides the ultimate glue. Stability is achieved, and even the gale winds of tradition do not overturn the new organizational behavior.

challenges to buy-in

The basic buy-in problem comes in step 4 and involves many issues besides those discussed in this book. But ideas, proposals, and plans can be shot down in all of the eight steps, potentially with a deadly effect on a change effort. So the material in this book applies to all aspects of a change process—from the articulation of a big opportunity facing an organization, which is shot down in step 1; to the idea of a great person to serve on the guiding coalition, which is shot down in step 2; to a very sensible idea for a change vision or strategy that is shot down in step 3; and so on through step 8.

But most of all, the material here has a special significance in step 4: communicate for buy-in.

The single biggest mistake that people make when trying to communicate a new vision of change, and strategies for achieving that vision, is under-communicating by a great deal. What seems like a lot of communication to those driving a change effort can, in fact, be woefully little, for perfectly understandable reasons.

Anyone playing an important role in a change effort will be talking about, attending meetings about, or writing about the change many hours each week. From this person's point of view, it can logically seem as if a huge amount of information has been compellingly communicated about the change vision and strategies. But up to, and during, step 4, the average person buried in an organization may be hearing about or participating in aspects of a large-scale change effort for an hour a month. Literally, an hour a month, or even less, which means less than 0.6 percent of a person's time on the job. Less than 0.6 percent! The other 99.4 percent of information and tasks and meetings and papers and e-mail—and, and, and totally overwhelms the 0.6.

Even if a manager or an employee feels a sense of urgency around a big opportunity and wants to help make something important happen, until he or she hears and buys into a direction for change and methods for getting there, what does the person do? Usually, the answer is little, except ask what is happening. If what people receive in return is a briefing at one meeting, the chances of them understanding all the work the guiding coalition has done, understanding fully the vision for change, understanding the strategies—buying into all this in their minds and hearts—is very close to *zero*. But top management often simply does not see or believe this truth, so the under-communication continues.

The second biggest mistake people make in their efforts to achieve buy-in to a smart vision and strategy—a direction for change that will propel the organization ahead, avoid dangers, and grab opportunities—is to communicate with all "head" and no "heart." When this mistake is made, as it often is, especially with the presentation of a long, analytical "business case," even if managers and employees come to understand a new vision and strategies, they will only understand in a detached, intellectual sense. The buy-in will lack the powerful emotional component that is needed to overcome inevitable obstacles on the road to success.

People in successful change efforts overcome these problems by communicating more and more often, and the communication is directed at both the head and the heart.

"More often" typically means using more means of communication. They don't just send out a few memos or merely have a segment at the annual management meeting devoted to the new vision and strategies. They relentlessly talk about change. They have a front-page article in every edition of the company newspaper. They put a change channel on desktops or use a "news" or "CEO" channel that already exists. They create kits for frontline supervisors to help them run a meeting for their people. They put up signs in factories. They create videos and send them around the firm.

Communication "at the heart," not just the head, means they use mechanisms with all communications that excite the feelings. They don't rely on analytically dry "business cases," no matter how thoughtful and rigorous. They use live events and video more than paper, because the former tends to express more emotion. We've seen companies put on plays, create competitive games, and urge the

CEO to be emotionally honest when he talks about the organization they need and the broader purpose of their work (i.e., not just increasing the stock price).

Where does our method fit into these scenarios?

The method described in this book does not—cannot—replace all the other buy-in tactics employed in successful large-scale change efforts. What it does is add a tool that is remarkably powerful and massively underutilized today.

The power of our method comes, first, from the fact that it captures people's attention to a degree that the vast majority of communication does not. The fact is, people don't look at the newspaper. They too often use their BlackBerries during speeches. They may give one more dull e-mail, among the fifty they receive in a day, twenty seconds of attention (literally). The very idea being communicated is not absorbed; much less are hearts and minds being won over. The method described here can score a 9 on that hypothetical 1–10 power scale and probably scores on average a 7. Other methods often score a 3. The difference between a 3 and a 7 in power rating cannot be overstated. Given the central role that attention plays in the ability to build support for a good idea, this difference alone can mark the difference between success and failure in creating buy-in.

Second, the power comes from the method's effectiveness in dealing with those maddening, tricky, generic attacks that inevitably arise in a large change effort, especially during step 4 (communicate for buy-in). It triumphs over a clever Pompus Meani or a very sincere, but destructive Allis Welli. It stops a Divertus Attenti. It shuts down a Lookus Smarti. These people, using confusion, delay, ridicule, and fear-mongering strategies, can so wound a change effort that it never achieves its potential. And from our research, we conclude that those sorts of people, and their antics, always exist—sometimes very visibly, sometimes more subtly behind the scenes.

Third, the method described here derives its power from its practical efficiency. We once saw a company create and perform again and again a play to communicate a new vision and strategy. It was incredibly creative. Most employees saw a live performance, typically in groups of a hundred. The play drew attention, informed the audience, and connected to hearts and minds. It also required six months to create and three months to give performances to people in twelve different offices. The total budget for actors, a screenwriter, travel, and staging, including outside vendors and the time absorbed by internal personnel, was well over $200,000. We think it was money well spent. But compare that with letting two carefully selected senior managers or executives in each office read about our method, giving them some coaching, time to prepare, and then time to use the method. By our crude math, the cost would be at most one-tenth the expenditure made on the play. Maybe one-twentieth.

Fourth, the method described here does not require only carefully selected senior executives. It can be used by virtually anyone, not just by those with great position power, wealth, status, or track records. Armed with our method, a twenty-three-year-old may not be able to face the top management committee. But he or she can be effective with many other people, especially junior-level employees in an organization, and this has exceptionally important implications. A CEO doesn't have to devote an unrealistic amount of his or her time trying to produce buy-in to a change vision and strategy. Executives do not have to devote an unrealistic amount of their time traveling from city to city giving a change speech (which, if not done well, will capture little attention and have little effect). Hundreds or even thousands of people throughout a medium-sized organization, much less a large one, can help with the buy-in problem and help in ways that are not just well-intended but also, in fact, effective. A very large number of people can also stop good ideas from being shot down in settings off the job: in schools, at home, in civic activities (like libraries!), and in many more situations.

These four pieces of the power equation, added together, can make the method described in this book a *very* unusual and *very* potent tool in any large-scale change effort. And from our observations, it is a much underutilized tool.

about the authors

JOHN P. KOTTER is internationally known and widely regarded as the foremost speaker on the topics of leadership and change. His is the premier voice on how the best organizations actually achieve successful transformations. The Konosuke Matsushita Professor of Leadership, Emeritus, at Harvard Business School and a graduate of MIT and Harvard, Kotter's vast experience and knowledge on successful change and leadership have been proved time and again. Most recently, Kotter has been involved in the founding of Kotter International (www.kotterinternational.com), a change leadership organization that helps global leaders develop the practical skills and implementation methodologies required to lead large-scale change in complex business environments.

Kotter has authored eighteen books, thirteen of them bestsellers. His works have been printed in over 120 languages, with total sales in excess of two million copies. His previous book, *A Sense of Urgency*, focuses on what a true sense of urgency in an organization really is, why it is an important asset, and how it can be created and sustained. For more information on his internationally acclaimed eight-step process for leading change, read his top bestsellers, *Leading Change* and *Our Iceberg is Melting*. They are key resources for any global leader in today's world of increasing change.

For more information, please visit www.kotterinterna tional.com.

LORNE A. WHITEHEAD is Leader of Education Innovation at the University of British Columbia, where he also holds the NSERC/3M Industrial Research Chair.

Whitehead holds more than one hundred applied physics patents and has received numerous awards for innovation leadership. Throughout his career he has served in executive and administrative roles in which he led the creation of new ventures and programs in both the private and public sectors.

Currently, his primary focus is helping universities to successfully apply recent discoveries that improve the effectiveness of teaching and learning. The latest spin-off from his laboratory is a system for piping sunlight into buildings in order to save electrical energy while providing people with natural illumination.

For more information, see http://www.physics.ubc.ca/profs/whitehead.html.